Creating Successful Business Systems: A Home Staging & Decorators Guide.

Free yourself through our proven systems.

Kristy Morrison

Creating Successful Business Systems: A Home Staging & Decorators Guide

Kristy Morrison
KristyMorrison0@gmail.com

The advice and recommendations in this book are the opinion of the author and should in no way replace the services of qualified real estate lawyers, real estate professionals, or mortgage professionals. Laws and regulations vary by area, making it important to consult with local professionals prior to purchasing or selling a property. Care has been taken to appropriately reference any books or quotes used in the writing of this work. The author and publisher welcome any information enabling them to rectify any reference errors and/or to attribute credit in subsequent editions.

Photos are the property of Capital Home Staging & Design.

BOOKS ARE AVAILABLE AT QUANTITY DISCOUNTS WRITE TO KRISTY MORRISON.
KristyMorrison0@gmail.com

ISBN: 978-1523724629
ISBN-13: 152371462X

Book Praise

"Kristy Morrison has now become the premier Home Staging Business Owner in North America. With her new book, Systems for Home Stagers and Decorators, she simultaneously shows you in great detail every single step it takes to build and run a successful and profitable home staging business while revealing her simplistic secret to success; systems that work.

In this book Kristy leaves no stone unturned and if you are up for the challenge, I would recommend you stop doing what you are doing right now and follow her lead. She is GIVING you the secret sauce. All you have to do is take it. What I have found with many home stagers is that they treat their home staging business like a hobby instead of a business. That is fine if you want a hobby. But if you are serious about running a successful six figure home staging business then this is the first step in doing just that. Follow Kristy Morrison and you will not only be following the leader of the Home Staging industry, but soon you will be following the future of the industry as well."

Karen Schaefer
Founder, APSD; The Association of Property Scene Designers
Colorado Springs, Colorado.

"Kristy's writing approach with direct and informative guidelines will help catapult your business to the next level. She takes the guesswork out of how to create a system based operation and gives the reader a clear and concise outline for success."

Jill Gargus
Simply Irresistible Interiors
Edmonton, Alberta.

"Kristy really nailed it with her latest book "Creating Successful Business Systems: A Home Staging & Decorators Guide". She tells you EVERYTHING on how to start and run you staging business effectively - from Employee Handbooks, Standard Operating Procedures, how to deal with difficult clients, how to hire staff and on and on. There is something (a lot!) for everyone here, whether you are a new business owner, in business for 5 years or a very experienced stager like me. Kristy shares her systems and forms for running a sleek, effective, efficient and profitable business. I highly recommend this book."

Michelle Minch
Moving Mountains Design Home Staging
Los Angeles, California.

―――――――――

"I met Kristy through her new business venture, and seeing the success she's been having in our business and her own staging business, I decided to read her new book. As an entrepreneur myself, I figured I might learn a thing or two on what kind of systems are implemented in other industries and hopefully get inspired to create some systems of my own in my field. Kristy's book was very inspiring and informative, I definitely got a lot more out of it than I would've thought! Her writing style is like sitting down and having a conversation with her over coffee. She explains everything really clearly and simply so the reader can implement her systems very easily and modify to their taste and personal situations. I would absolutely recommend this book to any business owner, but most especially to home stagers or decorators!"

Vicki Trudel
Entrepreneur
Ottawa, Ontario.

Dedication

I dedicate this book to all the stagers out there because without you I wouldn't have fire lit in my belly to inspire and educate others in an exciting industry. Together we stand united to transform spaces and help the lives of people we connect with daily.

Contents

Acknowledgements

To my amazing staging friends, this book is for you! Due to your outcry and massive support to one of my presentations at RESA, this book is dedicated to you all. From Canada to the USA, I have met many of you and admire each one of you for your passion and drive as well as your individual creativity. I wish you all great success and long bountiful business growth in an industry that challenges us not only physically, but also mentally.

Thanks to Catherine Lewis Brown for being a contributing author in this book. I admire your business knowledge and I love that you're so caring and willing to help stagers from all over. It's such an honour to have you contribute your wealth of knowledge for us all to learn and grow from. I am blessed to also call you a friend.

Todd McAllister, your fun personality is contagious. You have an amazing warehouse and unique storage systems. Thank you for allowing me to share your "Todd's Tidbit for Thursday" regarding warehouse tips. Your caring nature and willingness to share with this industry is inspirational.

To my Capital Home Staging & Design team, without your commitment to excellence I could not have built the company to its standing today.

Eric Bowen: You are my grounding sanity in my insane world. I Love You.

To my family Susan, Roy, Jonathan, Erika, Mila, Ocean: Another amazing adventure and I'm blessed to have your support along the way. Love you all.

Kristy Morrison

About This Book

This book is a unique, one-of-a-kind book. Designed specifically for stagers, decorators and designers to get a clear grasp on their business systems. Creating business systems is a daunting task that many of us put off each and every day because we dread writing the "system", it's no fun! Staging, designing and decorating spaces is the FUN part, transforming a home from drab to fab is what we all love the most.

After speaking at #RESACon2016 on setting up your business systems for success to a PACKED room, I received such positive and encouraging reviews. However, one trend kept popping up... "Where can I find more information on how to create systems easily?" A fellow stager at the convention, Ginny Truyens from Toronto, Canada, suggested over dinner, "Why don't you turn this into a book so we can work on our systems easily?"... BRILLIANT!!

On my 4hr flight back to Ottawa, I started the writing process to hammer this out as fast as I could for all those staging attendees who cried out for help so they could receive the book as soon as possible.

No matter how long you have been in business for, from day 1 to 10 years or more, this book will help you brain dump everything you've been storing to get it organized. That way you can officially have a true system for your company that will help make it scalable, measurable, duplicable, and possibly sellable. Be aware that the guidelines outlined in this book are subjective to different markets and may not comply with your employment or government laws.

Happy system-writing my friends!

Kristy Morrison   CEO – Capital Home Staging & Design

Kristy Morrison

Getting Started In The Office

Kristy Morrison

Why Bother Creating Systems?

The need for systems is a necessary requirement for all businesses around the world. A system makes your business unique, scalable and possibly even sellable in the future. Why create something that isn't positioned for a possible sale in the future?! We all start out thinking we will be stagers or decorators for the rest of our lives, but things happen. Maybe the industry loses its overall appeal, maybe a medical issue comes up and you can no longer be in your business. Whatever the case, you spent years of hard work, blood, sweat & tears (literally) building and developing something that clients recognize and use, so why not have it positioned for a possible sale or exit plan of your choosing?

The BEST time to start your business systems is when you open your business. This is the point where you have to create these systems and protocols anyway since they don't exist until then. If you are brand new to the industry, congratulations on the exciting adventure you are about to get into. This industry is huge and positioned for some massive growth in the coming years. If you are a veteran stager in the industry and you've been running your business without systems in place, then you deserve an award for keeping your sanity my friend!!! One of the hardest things to do is run a business, especially one with a team, and have no hard systems laid out for your company. However do not fret, I'm here to help and get you rolling so fast and easy that you will be wondering why you put this off for so many years.

Benefits of Taking the Time to Create Systems
✓ Having a clear direction on how to expand & grow over time.
✓ Being able to delegate tasks.
✓ Empowering your teammates to do what they do best.
✓ Increasing profit margins by identifying areas of financial drain.
✓ Creating a solid leverage model.
✓ Positioning yourself for possible future franchising.

- ✓ Owning a business that will be scalable and sellable.
- ✓ Setting up a strong exit plan.
- ✓ Keeping your SANITY.

This book is your guide to setting up clear systems in many areas of your business. Regardless of the level of business you want to achieve, this book will give you the tools to GROW with your business. Let's get started!

Tools you will need
-This Book
-Good Pen
-Quiet Room
-Passion

Items for larger binders
-Computer, Printer & Paper
-4'3 Ring Binder
-Dividing Tabs

LINK BONUS: I've spent nearly the last decade growing, systemizing, researching, testing and using different services / products. I've added recommended services and partners throughout the book and again in my resources section. Some of these affiliate links will provide me with a small commission or bonus for people who see the same value I saw and register themselves. I am telling you this upfront so you know 1000% that I am only providing these contacts purely for the fact that I personally use them; I'm not listing them because of a "bonus" they offer. I only recommend things I've put through my personal usage test.

Business SOP

The lifeblood of a business… at least it should be. A Standard Operating Procedure (SOP) outlines the Who, What, When, Where, Why, and How of any task within your business. We will be creating a TON of systems for your business together, but I need you to promise me that you won't get discouraged during this process. It seems hard, daunting, impossible and never-ending, but I PROMISE you that if you dedicate 30 minutes every day to filling out one SOP, then at the end of the year you will have 365 of them done and ready to go! This is called "The Compound Effect"; I also strongly suggest you read the book under that same title, written by Darren Hardy. The best part about creating business systems is to use the KISS method (Keep It Super Simple). Do not try and OVER create too many systems or you will get overwhelmed and inundated. Here is a general, not inclusive, list of SOPs we will be creating together.

Office Systems

- Office hours overview
    - Setting up office tools and services.
- Email templates
    - Booking Consultations
    - Scheduling Appointments
    - Follow up Emails
- Phone & voicemail systems
    - Answering calls
    - Response time
    - Scripts
- Appointment booking
    - Time blocking
- Pricing
    - Knowing your vacant numbers
    - Automating quotes to be 75% faster
- Employee handbook & benefits

- Outlining contracts required
- Accepting credit cards & payment forms

Job / Team Duties

- Home Stager
- Interior Decorator
- Office Manager / Administrator
- Warehouse Manager / Facilitator
- Student / Apprentice

Field Work Systems

- Occupied staging job overview
- Vacant staging job overview
    - Consultations
    - Inventory pulling system

Social Media

- Opportunity overview
- Creating attractive posts
- Scheduling system for automation

Warehouse / Storage Systems

- Determining when you need a warehouse
- Systems for best storage
- Inventory turnover / purging systems
- Tracking systems
- Safety protocols for warehouse

Hiring A Team

- Determine who to hire first
- Where to look for who (Skill List)
- Systemizing the interview process
- Pay systems

When it comes to creating job duties & systems for staff, we must separate duties based on the positions we are creating to subcategorize the tasks, even though we are the one's performing it all at first. When we start out in business, we are the sole proprietor, the admin, the stager, the creative person, the marketer, the presenter, the networker, the accountant, the everything operator essentially. We start by doing it all, but if we take the time to outline specific duties each position performs, it makes life so much easier when it comes to the hiring process.

First, we must identify & layout what your business identity & brand is. If you are new to business, you'll want to take a business development course, as that is an extra book on its own. However, this will get you well on your way if you are new. Your systems will always link to your business identity, and what you want to stand for and represent in your market place. When your identity matches your systems, a clear brand begins to develop and is respected by clients.

Kristy Morrison

YOUR OWN:
Business SOP

You can't create systems for your business if you don't know who you are or what you want. This is why we are going to take a quick moment to identify who you are, what your strengths are and what your goals are for your business.

Business Name:_____

Tag Line:_____

Vision, Mission, Values:

Do You Have A Logo? _____Yes _____No

Services You Provide (List All)

Your Preferred Target Market Is:
(In order of preference from 1-8, with 8 being MOST desired):

_____ Realtors
_____ Builders
_____ Home Owners
_____ Investors / Flippers
_____ Model Homes
_____ Property Managers
_____ VRBO Vacation Homes
_____ Other

Do You Have A Clear Pricing Outline? _____Yes _____No
*Market research is needed and I strongly suggest a pricing course if you marked no.

Do You Ever Want To Have A Team?
_____Yes _____No _____Unsure

What Specifically Do You LOVE To Do In Your Business Currently?

What Specifically Do You HATE To Do In Your Business Currently?

This is your list of items you'll want to delegate as soon as you possibly can! Focus on what you Love and what you are GOOD at!

What Do You Want To Be Known For In Your Market Place?

Do You Have A Specific Skill Or Talent You Can Capitalize On? If So, What Is It?

Ex: Painter, Artistic Painter, Pro Photographer, Great Sewer, Pillow Designer, Repurpose Queen, Etc.? If you can do something that someone else in your market isn't doing, use this as part of your unique selling proposition (USP).

Specific Notes About Your Business (Can Be Future Goals):

Sell What You Do By Building Your Brand!

Guest Author: Catherine Lewis Brown of…..

Getting Noticed!

When you start your staging business, you learn all about promoting yourself. Your end goal is to:

- attract the most amount of Ideal Clients, and
- motivate them to spend the most amount of money with you.

Don't be afraid to shout this from the rooftops, after all, if a business doesn't have paying customers, it isn't a business!

You reach your Ideal Client in tons of different ways:

- Keeping your website updated
- Printing a flyer
- Posting on social media
- Writing blogs
- Contributing as an expert
- Delivering a lunch and learn

The list goes on. These are all super ways and important elements to get your name out there and, when put together, create a brand.

The visual elements of our brand are the most obvious, and the ones we tackle first because they're almost tangible. They are also the simplest to use.

- Business name
- Font
- Colour

- Logo
- Graphic elements

Combine them with other parts of your brand and you have a real 'brand' identity!

What is a 'brand' and where does it fit in your business

Think about it this way, lots of successful stagers say they've never advertised their business, but they're still so busy. Why do you think this is? It's because the customer saw, read and/or heard something about the business that they liked. They were exposed to the stager's brand! Good advertising is built on the brand – the personality, the story, and the value of the owner and their business. The brand is not just about telling customers what you are selling. It tells them about you and your business – your story and what's important to you. THIS is what gets the customer to buy!

What are your favourite businesses (think local and small businesses too) and why do you choose to work with them? What attracted you to them over their competition? The answer will give you some insight into what people might look for when they're choosing you!

Why does it matters that your 'brand' is all about YOU

Being a staging business means that you stage houses, right? And you likely have inventory, a team of trained stagers, and a successful track record at making your clients money. You can be pretty sure that all stagers offer variations of these, but what separates you from other staging businesses (the competition) is YOU.

Why is this important? Because customers could work with any stager – you're all experts at what you do. But there is no one else like you, no one else that can do what YOU do the way you do because you each have your own story, your own values, your own promise to the client – you are one of a kind, and so is YOUR business. What you say, think, believe, love and do, is the basis of your brand!

> *Don't compare your business to others — there's no value to you comparing your inside to someone else's outside!*

What makes up your 'brand'

There are the obvious visual elements that make up your brand, like your logo. But there are many more that are unique to your business and that add real depth to your brand. These 'brand elements' are influenced by, and are a reflection of, you!

- What your business does
- What vision, mission and values your business is built on
- Who is your ideal client
- Where do you operate
- Where did you train
- What's important to you
- What value you bring

> *Go back to your business plan and you will find that several key pieces of your brand like these are already complete — no need to reinvent the wheel!*

Your core beliefs and passions also influence your brand. What matters to you, likely also matters to your Ideal Client.

- A cause or charity that means something to you
- The training that you recommend to new stagers
- Community events that are dear to you
- Other businesses you support, and that support you

> *Do a gut check when you're creating a service, a marketing message, a new tool, anything... and ask yourself, "Would I say this? Does this really reflect ME?"*

How to use your 'brand'

Now that you've looked deeper, you'll see that your business name and logo don't mean as much without the bigger, broader picture. It's kind of like adding colour, accessories and the lifestyle element to a room full of furniture! This is especially true when you think of attracting your Ideal Client. So dig deeper and take a second look at your business.

- Do the images on your website reflect your brand?
- Could you add more of YOU to your marketing?
- Do your business mission and values mirror what's important to you?

When you build a great brand that is about you, you attract your Ideal Client, which means you work with who you love, you deliver services to people who love them, and you build a business that YOU REALLY LOVE!!

Practical ways to include your brand everyday

There's lots you can include in building your brand, but there are some very easy, and no cost ways, to take the pieces of brand elements that you already have and build them into your everyday business.

> *Think about using email and Word templates, headers and footers, signatures, voicemail auto-responses – filling them in consistently using your logo, colours, fonts, phrases, terms, spellings, placements – and all of a sudden your brand is seen across your business! This is often referred as a Visual Identity Plan or, in the context of Word documents, a style sheet or guide. Although we usually think of large organizations having one, they can be SO helpful to a small business, and easily created! For example, you give this to your virtual assistant or even to someone you hired to create a brochure for your business.*

EASY PEASY and CHEAP ways to use your 'visual brand elements'

1. Choose one to two colours from your logo and use them to highlight key things, like headings or titles, in all your quotes, contracts, etc. – hit the 'more colours' in font, you'll be shocked.

    a. Think about using the colour in your headings and subheadings or your headers and footers. You can set these up as styles and in a template.

    b. Psst! Black is a default and pretty harsh, try dark grey instead.

2. Create a new 'body style' that includes a nice font that complements your logo (and that you'd like to look at every day)

    a. Choose a font that isn't Arial…

    b. Add a space after each paragraph that isn't a hard-return, like 6 point. Tip: Right click and select paragraph.

3. Think about the words you use every day. Do you refer to staging as showcasing, home staging or styling sometimes? Or the consultation versus the staging consultation? Make it easy for your customers by being consistent, pick one term and make it yours!

4. Use colour and font to create a graphic in your Word documents. For example, I write **mindYOURbizness** a lot, so I make it bold and then I use one of my colours to highlight it – adds more visual interest on the page, and people are drawn to the things that stand out!

5. Create a header and/or footer that you use for all your documents. You can even use the same one for your invoices. Place the graphics always in the same place, and use the same colours, e.g. make title no larger than the logo and always put the logo to the far left. Everything should say it's YOURS!

6. Write a couple of sentences that describe what you do and how you do it – make them part of your brand, too! You know when you have to write a profile? Be consistent and use these pre-made sentences or build on them, but keep the message, the feel, and the sentiment the same. Having these already written can save your bacon, copy and paste!

7. Select a few photos that have the look and feel that you love – they don't always have to be homes, if family is important to you, purchase stock photos that depict family – your choice should appeal to your Ideal Client!

8. Subscribe to motivational apps that deliver daily messages – include the ones that are particularly meaningful to you and will resonate with your Ideal Client!

> *It doesn't matter what your elements are (well, it kind of does… choosing wisely or paying an expert has its merits!), but most importantly, CONSISTENCY IS KEY!*

More ways to bring your brand elements together in one place!

- Post memes on social media with messages or quotes that are meaningful to you. I recommend using Canva.com (a great, easy, free online service!) to create the meme; adding that meaningful quote or message and your logo on one of your carefully selected photos.

- Write blog articles using the carefully selected photos, the colours, the keywords and most importantly, make your topic about something significant to you, like the cause or charity that means so much to you. And end with one of your pre-made sentences!

These are just a few ways to create consistency, but it's the consistency and the authenticity that comes from your brand when it's about you, that can be so powerful to keep the attention of and the loyalty, of your Ideal Client to you and your BRAND!

Create Your Own Easy Peasy Brand!

1. Your Brand Identity: What's your story, what came before?

2. Your Brand Values: What things are important to you, that you hold close to your heart? Think of values, opinions, view points, etc.

3. Your Branding (the visual elements): Pick a font that goes with your logo, is easy to read, and you like enough to see every day.

Pick two or three colours from your logo that you would happily use EVERYWHERE!

4. Your Branding Elements: Think of what's important to your brand like images, values, recognition, identity, etc.

List key words that you use in your business EVERY DAY and in ALL your communications, which are unique to you and your business.

5. Your Brand Promise: What solution are you selling, problem are you solving, pain point are you addressing?

Company Structure

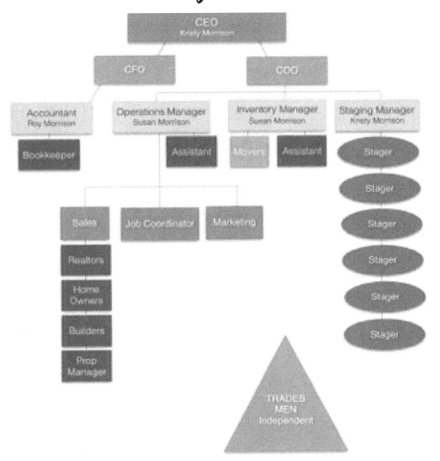

Every business should have a company flow chart outlining how they want to grow. Make this as BIG or as small as you'd like, and don't worry because this isn't set in stone, you can change it at any point. The chart above is the company structure I set up from day one. I knew I wanted to have a team so I created my structure quite large. Many of the tasks listed are fulfilled by a single person (usually the owner of the company), but giving them subcategories will allow you to identify where the duties will be separated in the business.

Owner

Office Operational Services

If you are a **NEW business** starting out and you haven't set up any of your business necessities (phone, internet, payment processing, energy, etc.), you'll want to check out the resources page for a *free quote* to get your business systems up and running, using well-known brands you already trust and love at wholesale / discounted pricing.

EXISTING businesses can benefit from dramatic savings also. I personally use ALL of these services to keep my business and home costs down. I've benefited from the following, which is why I became involved so I can help reduce costs to my fellow staging sisters & brothers.

Service	Monthly Home Savings	Monthly Business Savings	Annual Savings
Phone & Internet Bundle	**FREE** ($108.00)	**FREE** ($99.00)	$2484.00
Cell Phone *USA has FREE option	$50.00 (2 plans)	$50.00 (2 plans)	$1200.00
Merchant Processing	N/A	$92.00	$1104.00
TV	$5.00	N/A	$60.00
Hot Water Tank	$1.00	N/A	$12.00
Security	$0.00	$57.00	$684.00

Electricity / Gas / Solar	$50.00	30% at the end of 5 years	$660
	My Personal Annual Savings		**$6204.00**

What would you do with your new-found savings?

The BEST part of this entire program, beyond the proven savings, is with each service I register, a portion of my bills goes towards helping feed kids in North America through **Project Feeding Kids.** The program is partnered with the American and Canadian food banks and is localized to where the bills are registered. Having a recognition certificate posted on my office wall, guests can see our support to make a change and work towards ending childhood hunger in North America. I also have this amazing charity listed on my webpage so my clients know we are working towards making a difference. I registered all of my services, even those where savings were minor, because it still feels good to have an account registered to ensure a monthly contribution is made to the foundation.

Further details are listed in the resources section of the book.

SOPs for Job Duties

You'll want to write SOPs for only those that apply to your business. If some of these jobs overlap, that is fine – separate them first and when you hire someone for Office Manager / Warehouse Manager, merge the SOPs so they are clear on their duties.

- Business Owner (duties for each partner if you have partners in your business)
- Home Stager
- Interior Decorator
- Office Manager
- Warehouse Manager
- Assistant / Student

I've provided you with a copy of what my SOP looks like for HOME STAGERS on page 40. This is what I give to each staff member as a guideline of what their duties are while working with us. Many of the tasks may happen only on one job or none of them, but at least I have a clear list with all possibilities for my team to follow. Some of these duties you will not need your staff to perform. You'll want to think, "What do I want my _____(job position) to do for me?", that's the KEY to setting up your needs.

Job SOP generally need to contain the following information to ensure they are clear & concise. This should be specific to your business needs and what skills you want to hire in your company.

- Education / Credentials
- Memberships / Associations
- Experience
- Languages required
- Specific skills
- Job description

- Relationships
- Authority
- Special circumstances
- Performance indicators
- Pay rate

First we should establish a few key tasks each position is required to perform so beefing it up with the smaller tasks is easier. These are some required skills and tasks that I require from my team.

Business Owners
- Prepare marketing for the company.
- Hire, train & manage the team.
- Perform office & private meetings.
- Purchase inventory for the team.
- Evaluate all quotes before they are sent out.
- Plan company events & sponsorships.

Home Stagers
- Reliable & trustworthy.
- Self-motivated to complete tasks.
- Able to stand for long periods of time & be physically active.
- Driver's licence required.
- Ability to follow a set guideline of staging principles.
- Ability to communicate effectively with others.
- Must have certification from a staging school.
- Must also be able to work effectively in a team setting.

Interior Decorators
- Reliable & trustworthy.
- Self-motivated to complete tasks.
- Able to stand for long periods of time & be physically active.
- Driver's licence required.
- Ability to follow a set guideline of staging principles.
- Ability to communicate effectively with others.
- Must have certification from a decorating school.
- Must also be able to work effectively in a team setting.
- Strong knowledge of decorating principles.

- Able to source from multiple resources and stay within budgets.

Office Manager
- English speaking & writing skills required. French is an asset.
- Reliable & trustworthy.
- Self-motivated to complete tasks.
- Advanced knowledge of computer software.
- Ability to multitask on numerous projects at one time.
- Ability to effectively work in a fast-paced environment.

Warehouse Manager
- Ability to keep a large facility organized and clean.
- Ability to lift 25lbs over head with ease.
- Ability to take great care and pride in protecting inventory.
- Must be able to manage multiple jobs coming and going.
- Creating / tracking inventory storage solutions is an asset.
- Must be a self-starter and independent worker.

Assistant / Student Duties
- Ability to follow directions.
- Ability to anticipate the needs of the team.
- Must be able to stand for long periods of time.
- Must be able to lift 25lbs with ease.
- Must have a reliable method of transportation.

I've provided a copy of what our Home Staging job SOP looks like. This document is created and filed away for use only when I'm interviewing and hiring appropriate staff. Having this created from the beginning allows me to be prepared to train and hire someone faster than if I didn't have this document.

Now your turn to create a SOP… I have created a PDF page you can print out and use to start your SOP templates. You can find them at: www.KristyMorrison.com Books Section -Resources.

Remember, SOPs will change over time and that's ok, these are living, breathing tools that grow with us as needed.

Home Stager Job Template

Position:	Home Stager
Location:	Ottawa and the surrounding area
Department:	Design & Client Service
Job Code:	CAP-DEC-005 (Any code you like, you're making it up)
Reports to:	President, K. Morrison
Date:	October 2014
Approved by:	K. Morrison, President of **Capital Home Staging & Design.**

Credentials / Qualifications

Education:
* Completion of high school. (required)
* Completion of college/CEGEP/vocational or technical training of related program. (preferred)
* Diploma from a home staging course, interior decorating or design course or related programs. (preferred)

Other Credentials:
* Membership with RESA is an asset.

Experience:
* No experience required, Home Staging school training is mandatory.

Languages:
* Speak, Read and Write in English. (required)
* Speak, Read and Write in French. (asset)

Specific Skills:
* Reliability and trustworthiness are weighted extremely high;
* Self-motivation, drive, and passion for the design industry;
* Customer service oriented;
* Ability to understand client's ideas and turn them into reality;
* Sales driven to obtain decorating & staging appointments;
* Ability to lift 25lbs of furniture and boxes;
* Class G Driver's licence (required);

Job description

- Dress & act professionally at all times;
- Work directly with home owners & realtors in their home;
- Complete work for President Kristy Morrison directly or indirectly;
- Follow protocol outlined for each job to ensure the best results;
- Perform initial consultation presentation to home owners – education of service;
- Perform an in-home consultation for the home owners to keep;
- Have thorough knowledge on home staging techniques:
  - Appropriate selling colours
  - Target marketing to the right buyer
  - Good returns on investment for home owners
  - Traffic flow & focal points
  - Patterns & textures
  - Follow up emails to realtors
  - Etc.;
- Explain the importance of showcasing the home and why you should be brought back to perform the suggestions;
- Offer assistance to clients on getting outside help (painters, handymen, etc.);
- Work professionally with clients directly as well as being an intermediary between the real estate agents and clients;
- Provide head office with 2 articles per year for the newsletters – to get clients to know you;
- Create and maintain files;
- Create and maintain client information for the in-house database on Insightly.com,
- Maintain statistics and update the president on changes;
- Maintain and coordinate all schedules through Outlook and Google;
- Ensure proper follow up on jobs;
- Call new agents and giving them information packages for CHSD;
- Type and write correspondence, including: 'thank you' cards/emails;
- Gather marketing information packages and binding books;
- Maintain inventory list through proper communication with operations manager;
- Identify new processes for better efficiency;
- Assist the property stylist during showcasing / vacant staging;

- Anticipate the property stylist's needs and stay prepared;
- Some social media responsibilities may be required;
- May include: placing furniture and accessories, hanging artwork and drapery, making beds, ironing & steaming products, setting tables, vacuuming, mopping floors, dusting, and other general cleaning;
- Other duties as assigned.

Relationships

Internally, successfully relate with the president of the company. Externally, successfully relate with real estate agents, businesses, and general public.

Authority

This position has authority over the home staging assistant.

Special Circumstances

The incumbent will be required to travel in the Ottawa and surrounding areas at their own expenses. A T2200 form will be provided to assist with gas, car and home write-offs.

Performance Indicators

Performance indicators will include both quantitative and qualitative measures agreed by the President, HR Consultant and the Incumbent. Indicators may be market-based, business-based (ex: division profitability, budget control, days lost through industrial unrest, positive changes in employee commitment, job satisfaction and motivation) and individual basis (ex: performance as a leader and manager as assessed by superiors, peers, subordinates). Performance expectations and indicators will generally be defined on an annual basis. A formal performance appraisal will be conducted at least once a year.

Take the time to list all of the jobs that will be performed in your business and write out their SOP on the following pages.

1)_____
2)_____
3)_____
4)_____
5)_____
6)_____

YOUR OWN:
SOPs for Job Duties

Home Stager

Position: **Location:**   **Department:**   **Job Code:**   **Reports to:**   **Date Created:**   **Approved by:**

Credentials / Qualifications
Education:
-
-
-

Other Credentials:
-

Experience:
-

Languages:
-
-
-

Specific Skills:

Job Description

Relationships
Internally: _____

Externally: _____

Authority

Special Circumstances

Performance Indicators

<u>Interior Decorator</u>

<u>Position:</u> **<u>Location:</u>** **<u>Department:</u>** **<u>Job Code:</u>** **<u>Reports to:</u>** **<u>Date Created:</u>** **<u>Approved by:</u>**

Credentials / Qualifications

Education:
-
-
-

Other Credentials:
-

Experience:
-

Languages:
-
-
-

Specific Skills

Job Description

Relationships
Internally: _____

Externally: _____

Authority

Special Circumstances

Performance Indicators

<u>Office Manager / Administration</u>

<u>Position:</u> **<u>Location:</u>** **<u>Department:</u>** **<u>Job Code:</u>** **<u>Reports to:</u>** **<u>Date Created:</u>** **<u>Approved by:</u>**

Credentials / Qualifications

Education:
-
-
-

Other Credentials:
-

Experience:
-

Languages:
-
-
-

<u>Specific Skills</u>

Job Description

Relationships
Internally: _____

Externally: _____

Authority

Special Circumstances

Performance Indicators

<u>Warehouse Manager / Facilitator</u>

<u>**Position:**</u>
<u>**Location:**</u>
<u>**Department:**</u>
<u>**Job Code:**</u>
<u>**Reports to:**</u>
<u>**Date Created:**</u>
<u>**Approved by:**</u>

<u>Credentials / Qualifications</u>

Education:
-
-
-

Other Credentials:
-

Experience:
-

Languages:
-
-
-

<u>Specific Skills</u>

Job Description

Relationships
Internally: _____

Externally: _____

Authority

Special Circumstances

Performance Indicators

<u>Assistant / Student Duties</u>

<u>Position:</u>
<u>Location:</u>
<u>Department:</u>
<u>Job Code:</u>
<u>Reports to:</u>
<u>Date Created:</u>
<u>Approved by:</u>

<u>Credentials / Qualifications</u>
Education:
-
-
-

Other Credentials:
-

Experience:
-

Languages:
-
-
-

<u>Specific Skills</u>

Job Description

Relationships
Internally: _____

Externally: _____

Authority

Special Circumstances

Performance Indicators

SOP Title

Position: **Location:**   **Department:**   **Job Code:**   **Reports to:**   **Date Created:**   **Approved by:**

Credentials / Qualifications

Education:

  -
  -
  -

Other Credentials:

  -

Experience:

  -

Languages:

  -
  -
  -

Specific Skills

Job Description

Relationships
Internally: _____

Externally: _____

Authority

Special Circumstances

Performance Indicators

Employee Handbook

Now that our SOPs are created for each current job, as well as future jobs, it's time to work on what your employee handbook should be like. Having an employee handbook is a necessity in a business that will have employees. If you currently do not have any employees, you can skip this step, however keep it in the back of your mind for when you do decide to start hiring a team.

Each province/state will have different employee rules, so please do your research on local government sites to see what rules are mandatory for staff-based businesses. Our employee handbook is about 10 pages and outlines all terms as far as how I expect my team to operate overall.

Your handbook topics will generally include the following:
- Family medical leave policies
- Equal employment & non-discrimination policies
- Workers compensation policies
- Company's history
- Paid time off policy
- Employee conduct
    - Hours of work / attendance & punctuality / overtime
    - Behaviour standards
- Pay & Promotions (ensures it's clear to employees what to expect)
    - Salary/ pay outline / raises
    - Leave & Benefits (holidays / vacations / sick leave / personal leave / military leave / jury duty / separation / etc.)
    - Reimbursement of expenses
    - Return of property owned by the company
    - Outside employment terms (non-compete / non-disclosure)

In your employee handbook, you will want to establish the CULTURE you are looking for within your company. I have it listed as 'company's history'. If you are new, then let's outline what we want in our company. Most of this we already did in our opening with your business identity (woohoo, bet you didn't expect to be ½ done this part now, eh!?) This part of the workbook is best kept in an exclusive employee handbook / duo-tang. Keep multiple copies available for your team to reference points as often as they want.

Utilize local government / employment webpages to ensure your terms and policies are legal and properly outlined for your market.

Employment links for most of our **Canadian** province.

Alberta	www.work.alberta.ca
British Columbia	www.labour.gov.bc.ca
Manitoba	www.gov.mb.ca
New Brunswick	www2.gnb.ca
Newfoundland	www.gov.nl.ca
Nova Scotia	www.novascotia.ca
Ontario	www.labour.gov.on.ca
PEI	www.gov.pe.ca
Quebec	www.cnt.gouv.qc.ca
Saskatchewan	www.saskatchewan.ca

Employment links for most of our **American** states.

Alabama	www.employmentlawhandbook.com
Arizona	www.azleg.gov
Arkansas	www.labor.ar.gov
California	www.dir.ca.gov/dlse/
Colorado	www.colorado.gov/
Connecticut	www.ctdol.state.ct.us/
Delaware	dia.delawareworks.com/
Florida	www.stateofflorida.com/
Georgia	www.dol.state.ga.us
Idaho	www.labor.idaho.gov
Illinois	www.illinois.gov
Indiana	www.in.gov
Iowa	www.iowadivisionoflabor.gov
Kansas	www.dol.ks.gov/Laws/
Kentucky	www.labor.ky.gov/
Louisiana	www.employmentlawhandbook.com/
Maine	www.maine.gov
Maryland	www.dllr.state.md.us
Massachusetts	www.mass.gov/
Michigan	www.employmentlawhandbook.com
Minnesota	www.dli.mn.go

Mississippi	www.mdes.ms.gov/
Missouri	labor.mo.gov
Montana	dli.mt.gov/
Nebraska	dol.nebraska.gov/
Nevada	www.laborcommissioner.com/
New Hampshire	www.nh.gov/labor/
New Jersey	lwd.dol.state.nj.us
New Mexico	www.blr.com
New York	www.labor.ny.gov
North Carolina	www.nclabor.com
North Dakota	www.nd.gov/labor/laws/
Ohio	www.ohio.gov
Oklahoma	www.ok.gov
Oregon	www.oregon.gov
Pennsylvania	www.portal.state.pa.us/
Rhode Island	www.dlt.ri.gov
South Carolina	www.llr.state.sc.us/
South Dakota	www.dlr.sd.gov
Tennessee	www.blr.com
Texas	www.twc.state.tx.us/
Vermont	www.labor.vermont.gov/
Virginia	www.doli.virginia.gov

Washington D.C.	www.does.dc.gov/
Washington	www.lni.wa.gov
West Virginia	www.wvlabor.com/
Wisconsin	www.dwd.wisconsin.gov
Wyoming	www.wyomingworkforce.org

Employee Benefits

Holidays
On all stat holidays, the company will be closed. Should an "urgent" request come in for an appointment due to scheduling with the clients, we will put a call out to all stagers requesting this time off. It will be up to each stager to determine if they would like to take the job or not. Booking will happen on a first come first approved basis.

Sick Time
Full time staff are entitled to 5 sick days per year.

Vacation
Full time staff are entitled to 2 weeks of paid vacation time. Vacation time must be booked at least 1 week in advance to ensure proper scheduling and company coverage. Vacation time is limited during peak season of March-June. Head office has the right to refuse time off to any employee should it not suit the company schedule. Employee may select an alternative date for approval.

Pay Schedule
Each team member is paid out twice a month, on the 15th & the 30/31st. Time sheets are required immediately upon the 2-week cycle so accounting can properly prepare everyone's pay at the same time.

Raises
Pay increments are reviewed annually and are based not only on employee performance, but overall company performance.

Pay Chart
Each employee has their own pay schedule based on position duties, length of service within the company, etc.

Tax Write-Offs
During tax season we will provide a T2200 form to allow employees to deduct common expenses we do not cover. *Information specifically for Ontario, Canada.*

Punctuality
If you're "On Time", you're late. If you're late, then you're fired, based on a 3 strikes policy. *This is a non-negotiable in my company, I hate when people do not respect other people's time.*

Staff Meetings Are: __X__ Mandatory Paid
_____Mandatory Unpaid
_____Optional

In Canada, all staff members need to be paid a minimum of 3hrs per shift, so we hold 3hr staff meetings once a month.

Hiring Practices
How do you hire in your company? Many labour laws require equal opportunity and non-biased judgement of staff. Use the upcoming space to outline how you will advertise or make any announcements of employment opportunity.

Standards of Conduct
This is the overview on how you expect the staff to work and conduct themselves on the job site. This generally outlines terms related to serious offences, such as sexual harassment, consumption of alcohol, possession of illegal substances, working while under the influence of drugs or alcohol, etc.

Do you have a smoking policy? Provide an overview of what you determine is an "improper work habit", including failure to record overtime, extended breaks, unauthorized taking of company supplies, using the company's computer system for personal use during work hours, improper recording of work hours, being frequently absent or tardy, disregard of personal appearance / hygiene, etc.

Work Hours
Operational hours for office and stagers are outlined. Since we are an industry of irregular hours, you will want to outline those terms / fluctuating times here.

	Mon	Tues	Wed	Thurs	Fri	Sat	Sun
Office	9-4p	9-4p	9-4p	9-4p	9-4p	Closed	Closed
Stagers Consults	9-9p	9-9p	9-9p	9-9p	9-9p	9-3p	Closed
Stager Vacants	9-12p	9-12p	9-12p	9-12p	9-12p	Closed	Closed

Employee Status
Full Time Staff: outline what a full time staff member looks like; generally 40hrs a week & entitled to company benefits.

Part Time Staff: outline what part time staff members look like; generally working less than 30hrs a week on a regular basis. Are they eligible for any company benefits?

Anniversary Dates
What is an anniversary date? Ours is defined as an employee's first day on the job with the company.

Performance Reviews & Appraisals
Here you will want to outline what the probationary / training time period is for your company as well as what happens when the probationary period ends. You will also want to outline performance reviews that will be conducted for your company

and how often. I choose to do a mid-point check-in every 6 months and a final year-end review so the team can learn where to improve and where we really love what they excel in.

Salary & Payment Reviews

Your staff will want to know when you will be evaluating their payment terms. This will allow your staff to be prepared for reviews and to know that these are not guaranteed. Staff are not automatically entitled to annual pay raises; these are based on performance and company profits.

Grievance & Discipline Procedures

This topic is always a hard one to outline. I really used my local employment office to help outline these terms for my company as far as what is a fair standard practice. Overall, how will you handle staff that are initiating a grievance process, where they complain or protest for unfair treatment, or how will you discipline staff should they do something wrong while working? Here is an example of how to deal with issues in a 4-step process, so that these issues are clearly outlined each time and staff are disciplined as necessary. This is tracked with a disciplinary employee form, example seen page 65.

a) **First Conference** (verbal reminder):

• Performance standards or behavioural expectations of employee will be reviewed.

• Employee's commitment to meeting standards will be obtained.

b) **Second Conference** (written reminder):

• Management will emphasize why problem must be resolved.

• Written solution to the problem will be filed.

• Employee's commitment to meeting standards will be obtained.

c) **Third Conference** (employee decision day):

• A leave day with pay (not to exceed 1 day) will be granted so employee can decide if he or she wants to commit to solving the problem.

• Employee's commitment to meet standards will be obtained or employee will be terminated.

d) **Termination**

Disciplinary Form

Name: _____

Employee Start Date: _____

Position: _____

Date of Verbal Warning:_____

Verbal Warning Issued: _____

Reasoning: _____

_____

Date of Written Warning #1:

_____

Written Warning Issued:_____

Reasoning: _____

_____

Copy of Written Warning Attached: _____Yes   _____No

Date of Written Warning #2:

_____

Written Warning Issued:_____

Reasoning: _____

_____

Copy of Written Warning Attached: _____Yes   _____No

Result of Written Warning #3: ___Probation ___Termination

Copy of Written Warning Attached: _____Yes _____No

Dismissal Terms
These will be VERY specific to employment laws as far as how to handle dismissal of an employee. Generally after probationary term, staff are entitled to some benefits. If an employee **QUITS**, they are usually not entitled to any company benefits. If they are **FIRED** with cause, they are not entitled to any company benefits. If they are **LAID OFF** due to lack of work or not being needed anymore, they are entitled to specific termination benefits.

For example, as per the Ontario Employment Law:
Anyone employed past probationary period but less than one year, an employee may be eligible for written notice of termination as follows;

Employed	Notice of termination
Less than 1 year	1 week notice
More than 1year	2 weeks notice
Employed 3-5 years	3 weeks, plus 1 additional week for each additional year of employment, to a maximum of 8 week's notice.

Rest Periods
This section will outline breaks associated with work duties. This is also strictly regulated by local employment authorities.

An example from my Ontario Market, full time salary employees are paid on the basis of 8 work hours per day. This includes a 0.5-hour lunch break and two 15-minute breaks throughout the day.

For part-time employees, the following will be used as a guide for breaks (paid) and lunches (unpaid):

Break Outlines

Hours Worked	Breaks
0-4.5 hours	Entitled to no breaks.
5-6 hours	Entitled to one 15-minute break & 30 min lunch.
6.5+ hours	Entitled to two 15-minute breaks & 30 min lunch.

Some staff will want to skip their two 15-min breaks to take a 1hr lunch or leave 1hr early. This is not legal and if an employer is caught not enforcing the break laws, they will be fined. Again, each state and province will have different rules and regulations so be sure to know what they are in your area and enforce them.

Overtime
In this section you will want to outline your policies regarding overtime. Do you allow staff to work overtime? How are they compensated? Is it accumulative? Can they bank overtime and save it for paid time off years down the road? Many companies don't offer overtime, and if they do, the time off must be taken within 6-12 months or they lose it. This protects companies from their staff banking hours over 20 years, and then taking paid time off for 6+ months, which tends to deplete resources and funds for many small to medium-sized businesses.

Pay Periods
When are staff paid and how are they paid? Cheque, direct deposit, cash? What happens to an employee's cheque when a pay period lands on a statutory holiday?

Employee Benefit Plans
Do you offer employee benefit plans? Health insurance plans? Most group benefit plans need to have more than 1 full time employee working in the workplace to be eligible.

Public Holidays
List all holidays that the company is closed during the year.

Paid Vacation
All employees are entitled to paid vacation time. How are they paid? When must they take their payment? Do you have mandatory vacation times? Some companies will have a one week mandatory vacation that counts towards the staff's vacation time around Christmas when business is slow. Employers are allowed to dictate "black out days" for employee vacations, and when the terms are laid out upfront, it reduces confusion and issues in the future with staff.

Sick or Personal Leave
After the probationary period, how do you handle sick or personal leave? For my company, employees are permitted 5 sick days of absence per year with no pay. Overall, sick days cannot exceed 20 days in a 3 year time period. You will also want to have terms listing the following life scenarios & what you allow:
    -Maternity / parental leave
    -Bereavement leave
    -Leave of absence (long or short)
    -Jury Duty / Voting

Educational Assistance
Do you assist staff with additional training? Do you pay for training in full or partially? Are staff required to pay back the cost of training if they leave your company on their terms? Within a certain time frame? How do you approve specific courses for staff? Will they submit a form requesting to take a class or can they register for anything and you will pay them back? There is no right or wrong answer here, just decide what is right for you.

Personal Telephone Calls, Emails, and Visitors
How do you handle staff constantly on their phones? Do you limit this to just break times? What do you expect of your staff when it comes to personal time?

Personal Expenses

What do you, as a company, pay for and what do you expect your staff to pay for? Will they pay for gas? Their own office supplies? How will they be reimbursed if necessary?

Gifts

Are staff allowed to accept gifts from customers?

Security

What security systems do you have in place? All staff in my company MUST keep their cellphone on them during an appointment, on silent mode, and only use it if there's an emergency situation. All staff are scheduled in Google calendar and must text the office when they are DONE a job to confirm they are ok.

Dress Code

Do you require staff to wear a uniform? How should they dress? When it comes to setting up your employee handbook, there is no right or wrong, as long as it is within the legal limits of your jurisdiction. This is very custom to your wants for each team member. When I created my employee handbook, I always thought on a large scale future, *"If I had 20 staff members, how would I want each of them to conduct themselves if I wasn't around?"*

Kristy Morrison

YOUR OWN:
Employee Handbook

This is an overview section that should be compiled in its own binder for staff to easily reference.

Company's History

My Company Was Established In:_____

We work with _____(who)
to provide _____(what)
& _____(why)

E.g.: We work with realtors to provide vacant transformations so homes will sell in 15 days as opposed to the average 120 days for an empty unstaged home.

Your Vision, Mission Value: Already written out in your business identity section of this book.

Employee's Behaviour

This section will outline how you want your staff to dress, act and ultimately behave at all times, especially when you are not around, because the team is ultimately the make or break point of your business as you grow. While you are working through these guidelines, be as specific as you possibly can.

Dress code:

E. g.: Employees must wear black shirt and pants, no jeans, and closed-toe shoes. Any employee wearing flip flops, ripped jeans, low-cut shirts or anything with political or religious outlines will be written up and sent home.

Profanity / Culture:

E.g.: If a staff member is caught using profanity in the workplace in regards to, but not excluding to, discrimination based on age, gender, race, sexual orientation, religion, political views, etc. will not be tolerated and staff member will be terminated on the spot.

Mandatory Expectations of Employees:

E.g.: Each employee must conduct themselves in a professional manner in which they are respectful, curious, helpful and knowledgeable on topics they were hired for. All employees will uphold the guidelines listed throughout the employee handbook at all times, on and off company hours, as brand reputation will carry on into our personal lives and must be respected in a social media world.

Will your team be Staff or Independent Contractors?

_____Staff   _____Independent Stagers.

(For ease of this book, I will use the word Staff as your team, even if they are Independent Contractors.)

How will you pay your staff?	___Salary ___Hourly ___Per job ___Other			
Will your staff earn overtime pay?	___Yes	___No	___Time off	
Will you offer regular raises to staff?	___Yes	___No	___Based on profits	
When will you pay your staff?	___Daily	___Weekly	___Bi-Weekly	___Monthly
Do you require non-disclosure / non-compete agreements?	___Yes	___No		

*Note: Be sure to confirm your desires are legal in your state or province.

Kristy Morrison

YOUR OWN:
Employee Benefits

Holidays:

Sick Time:

Vacation:

Pay Schedule:

Raises:

Pay Chart:

Tax Write-Offs:

Punctuality:

Staff Meetings Are:_____Mandatory Paid
_____Mandatory Unpaid
_____Optional

Hiring Practices:

Standards of Conduct:

Work Hours:

	Mon	Tues	Wed	Thur	Fri	Sat	Sun
Office							
Stagers Consults							
Stagers Vacant							

Employee Status:

Anniversary Dates:

Performance Reviews & Appraisals:

Salary & Payment Reviews:

Grievance & Discipline Procedures:

Dismissal Terms:

Rest Periods:

Overtime:

Pay Periods:

Employee Benefit Plans:

Public Holidays:

Paid Vacation:

Sick or Personal Leave:

Educational Assistance:

Personal Telephone Calls, Emails, and Visitors:

Personal Expenses:

Gifts:

Security:

Other:

Office & Administration SOPs

In this section, we will get the company's inner workings all ironed out. From responding to incoming requests to coordinating your growing team, your office is the HUB of your business. If the terms and contents are not clearly defined, then the busier you get, the more confused you will be on what you laid out, because as human beings, they say we can only remember seven things at a time! I can tell you I feel like I'm constantly thinking of a million things, but apparently it's only a measly seven.

Office Checklist of Created SOPs
- Office Hours / Response Timing
- Answering Phones & Emails
- Email Templates
- Booking appointments / Tracking
- CRM – Client Relationship Management System
- Google Calendar Scheduling
- 12-Step Folder System Overview
- Payment & Refunds Outline
- Invoicing protocol
- Occupied Consultations – Contract
- Realtor Forms
- Vacant Forms
- Scheduling of Affiliates (movers, photographer, etc.)

The first thing we need to establish is your operating hours. When will your office be open and receiving incoming calls? I strongly suggest setting expectations from the beginning because changing this later on as you grow can be difficult for some regular clients. Will the office hours be different from the stagers' hours? Remember, our office is opened Monday – Friday from 9am – 5pm and closed on weekends, but stagers are available Monday – Friday from 9am – 9pm, and Saturday from 9am – 3pm. Also, you'll want to identify how fast you'll respond to incoming calls & emails.

Next is our phone script for answering calls. This will allow a consistency and a brand to develop when it comes to growing your company.

> *"Thank you for calling Capital Home Staging & Design, Samantha speaking, how may I assist you?"*

Quick, simple, and to the point, our office administrator will be answering the phones consistently in the same manner during business hours.

Our voicemail script for after hours or when our phone lines are busy goes like this:

> *"Thank you for calling Capital Home Staging & Design. Your call is important to us, please leave your name, phone number and details regarding your call, and we will get back to you as soon as possible. Please note our office hours are Monday through Friday from 9am to 5pm."*

I forget which stager I got this great quote from, but ever since I added it to my webpage, we've reduced the amount of discount requests. It sets the tone that we know our pricing and value are appropriate for what we are known to deliver.

> *"Please note our service fees are a reflection of results and value you can expect when working with us."*

All of our office hours and terms are listed on our webpage under the "Contact" tab.

Here you can see we have clearly identified the following:
- Office phone number
- Office & accounting email address
- Mailing address
- Warehouse address
- Hours of operation (office & stagers)
- Holiday hours

(Go directly to our webpage to see larger.
www.CapitalHomeStagingAndDesign.ca)

Kristy Morrison

YOUR OWN:
Office & Administration SOPs

Office Hours: _____

Stager Hours: _____

Holiday Hours: See Employee Handbook for closed office hours' list.

All Calls Will Be Responded Within (timeframe): _____

All Emails will Be Responded Within: _____

Answering Calls Script:

After Hours Voicemail Script:

Other Office Notes:

Kristy Morrison

Avoiding Client Issues

This hot topic is a hard one for our industry because as a stager, we give clients what they need, and they literally should have no say in what we deliver because they are not trained to know what the home's needs are. Most customers confuse decorating with staging, and make requests on how the furniture should be placed or what the colour scheme should be, or even sometimes, when something is brought in, they will request it to be replaced with another piece that they like. Well, that is NOT how the home staging industry works, and if you are going to survive with your sanity, you'll need to start by setting some expectations with your customers.

The best way to set customer expectations is upfront. When I meet with a potential client for a vacant quote, I use my list of vacant questions (see vacant SOP section), and at the end before I leave, once I have all my information, I ask two very important questions:
1) Are you wanting to sell fast or stage cheap?
2) Are you willing to let us have full control on what goes into this home to have a proper set up?

If the home owners answer "cheap" to the first question and "no" to the second question, then I will advise them right on the spot that we are not the company for them as our goals do not align. Some of you may be having heart palpitations at the thought of being so forward with the client, however, in my years of experience, the more posture and confidence YOU have, the more confidence you instill in the home owners, and the more likely they are going to spend more with you. If they truly are looking for the cheapest staging job, you should let it go onto someone that is willing to work hard for peanuts. By focusing on the type of clientele you desire, you will allow your company to be efficient and clear to your prospects that you are not desperate for their work and are not willing to do just anything to get it.

Real World Example:

A few years ago, my office received a call to stage a home 30 minutes away from our office. Susan, our office manager, performed her necessary office duties, asking this prospect questions, and none of them matched up. Susan was asking for more information about the vacant home and the prospect responded with, "Oh, we are not the owners, we are managing the property while the clients are away on vacation; they are trying to TEST the market for sale. The home is of an average size in a desired neighbourhood. I would like to stage the living and dining rooms and the master bedroom." Susan advised that we do not stage JUST the rooms that the prospect is requesting, and that they will require a proper consultation to determine the home's needs. She proceeded by telling the prospect that our consultation fee is xxx and is non-refundable, but if they hired us for the job, that fee would be applied to the grand total at the end of the staging job. The prospect agreed and booked a consultation.

Since we had a trainee at the time, I accompanied her to the home, and as soon as we pulled up into the laneway, I determined this was NOT an "average home", this was in fact a luxury mansion. FLAG ONE: client lied about the size of the home.

Next, we met the prospect and did a tour of the home. The massive library / living room, family room, dining room, large eat-in chef's kitchen, and 5 bedrooms on the 2nd floor, all with their own bathrooms. Once the tour was done, I asked the client what the budget was, and she responded, "$2,000. We only want to stage 1 living room, 1 dining room and the master bedroom." All the other kids' rooms had beds (ugly ones for that matter), and she was willing to bring in her OWN items to stage those rooms for free, while we staged the other 3 rooms. This lady was clearly trying to dictate how WE, as a company, were supposed to operate. I advised this client that we only stage the necessary amount of rooms required to get interest in a home, which in this case were ALL decision-making rooms, so 2 living rooms, 2 dining rooms, the kitchen with island-seating, 4 bathrooms, the master bedroom, and 2 of the 4 kids' rooms. I also advised that the quote would be starting at $6k, but I wouldn't know the exact price until I got back to the office and really put pen-to-paper to figure this one out.

The client agreed and I got to work. I spent five hours quoting the property because I could tell she was a difficult client and I wanted to be 200% accurate on the quote sent. The client responded immediately with threatening statements about how I was a scam artist, charging a consultation fee and not being able to service a client the way they wanted. To smooth the waters, I called and advised her that I had been upfront the entire time, stating the consultation fee was non-refundable, and we would not stage just the rooms she was requesting, we would stage the rooms we deemed appropriate to get the job done.

Long story short, even though we were upfront with how we work, she tried to twist and turn the process the entire way. Ultimately, I ended up having to refund her our consultation fee for her to remove the negative posts she had put on social media. Sometimes cutting ties fast is easier than fighting them. Can you imagine how this job would have turned out if we had not been upfront in how we operate? The inventory would probably have been scrutinized, the placement, the colour scheme, the renewal fees, everything! The bottom line to the entire project was that she never let us talk to the owners of the home, so we are glad we walked away from this job early on.

Here's our upfront system for avoiding customer issues:

1. Occupied Stagings:
    i. We **don't** rent accessories for sanitary reasons.
    ii. We **do** use their existing items or will perform personal shopping services so they can own the products after.
    iii. We **don't** perform consultations outside our written system.

2. Vacant Stagings:
    i. We **don't** perform
        i. Partial stagings,
        ii. Virtual stagings,
        iii. Budget stagings.
    ii. We **do** fully stage decision-making rooms with enough furniture and decor to transform the room.
    iii. We **don't** allow clients to have input in the products & inventory used.
    iv. We **do** create a custom plan for each property. We are a staging company first and a rental company last.
    v. We **don't** discount our staging services at any time.

3. Assistants:
    i. We **don't** allow non-staff to participate in the staging process.

4. Warehouse:
    i. We **don't** allow non-employees to enter the warehouse.

Outline your do's and don'ts for your company

Occupied Stagings

Vacant Stagings

Assistants

Warehouse

So what do you do when you've set client expectations and they are still not happy with what you're delivering? You'll need to evaluate each situation case by case. Let's review some common issues & how we have set up our company to deal with them in a step by step manner.

Customer isn't happy with the staging look.

1. Remind them that staging is different than decorating, and it's normal to not like the results because they are no longer our desired target buyer.

2. Advise the client that they have the option, as per the contract, to have you remove the staging inventory immediately, however, refunds are not offered as our services have been delivered in full according to the terms outlined. (This is why it is worth having a lawyer draft up an iron-clad contract so you can confidently stand behind your company terms.)

3. If client complains on social media, offer a 50% refund if they remove the comments immediately. Only refund the client after the post has been removed and not before. This is a term you'll want to consider because if you are using a 3rd party supplier, they will not refund you the rental fees. I can only offer the 50% refund because I own my inventory and it's not a financial loss for me like it would be if I had paid someone for those rented items. Also remove your items from the home ASAP.

Customer isn't happy that a room wasn't staged and they thought it was supposed to be.
1. Politely review the staging proposal and rental agreement where it outlines the rooms to service. This will identify that the specific room they wanted wasn't listed. If it was listed, this is your fault and you'll need to deliver it at your own cost and chalk it up to a learning experience.

Customer wants a bunch of inclusions for free.
1. Advise the client that there is a cost to having inventory used in the home and it must be compensated for.
2. If they are adamant, I will toss in a bathroom or laundry room staging. Beyond that, we will refuse a job with pushy clients.

Dropbox – Everyone Needs It

Many of you have probably heard of Dropbox. For those of you who haven't, in my resources page, I have a link to get started where you can earn additional storage for free by sending referrals to your network.

Getting set up is very easy and self-explanatory. Where to start filing documents as they are being created is the difficult part. I use Dropbox to store ALL of my company files so I can access them anywhere in the world. First, go to www.dropbox.com and click on "Try it free", filling out the necessary information.

Because it is web / cloud-based, you can have access to all of these documents with any computer, smart phone or tablet that can connect to the internet, anywhere in the world. I choose to keep all of my documents here because when I am away on vacation, if a team member asks me where a specific document is, I can easily send it to them or walk them through the area to get it. Doing this on a desktop computer hard drive is nearly impossible, especially when it's locked up in your house while you are away.

Benefits of Dropbox

- Give visibility control on specific documents to specific teammates.
- 24/7 online access to files that sync seamlessly.
- External sharing links make it easy to open and use documents.
- Peace-of-mind system back up. If your computer crashes or dies, all of your documents will be safe in the "cloud".
- Excellent referral program so you can obtain 17GB of storage for free, just by sharing with your network.
- Hundreds of thousands of app integrations to work with many well-known systems like Vimeo, Auto Cad, & more.

Here's an example of my main folder categories and the documents created, to help get you organized with your documents.

1) Company overview & regulations
   i. About Capital Home Staging & Design
   ii. Company Regulations
   iii. Safety & Security Protocols
2) Employee Policies & Benefits
   i. Student Protocol
   ii. Staff Forms (time-off sheets, etc.)
   iii. Job Descriptions
   iv. Hiring & Firing Forms
   v. Employee Handbook
3) Job "How-To"
   i. Occupied Home Staging
   ii. Vacant Home Staging
4) Inventory Management
   i. Inventory Codes
   ii. Suppliers Price List
5) Operations (office)
   i. Ordering Files (business cards, brochures)
   ii. CRM Set Ups
6) Marketing
   i. All flyers I ever created & marketing pieces
7) Payment & Agent Forms
   i. Credit Card Form
   ii. Realtor Agreement Form
   iii. Occupied Home Staging Contract
   iv. Vacant Home Staging Contract
8) Awards & Submissions
9) Logos
10) Testimonials
11) Accounting
   i. Private team info about employment contracts
   ii. Pricing Structure (evaluated yearly)
12) Private Business Documents
   i. Master Business Licence +/- Incorporating Papers

Company Email Templates

Next, we need to create email templates for each service you provide so that, should you be "out of office", someone can access these templates and business will proceed as usual. We already established business and stager hours of operation, now we have to simplify each job that could be booked through your company by using email templates.

I use a 3-email template system so I'm not overwhelmed with too many email templates. The only thing I adjust is the terminology used in the email for home owners, realtors and investors. My first template is the SALES template; this generally will provide prospects with a written overview of our value because we DO NOT want people to compare us based on price, we want them to compare us based on the value we provide and the level of detail in our specific service. We have had great success with selling clients online by providing them with a clear price and a detailed list of what they get for that price. If I am quoting a vacant job, I outline our company stats, our proven sales from a recent job and I provide a range of prices based on the information the home owner has given me. From there, I offer to book a paid consultation appointment to firm up the price and I let them know, should they proceed, we will apply the consultation fee to the full staging job. I've chosen to do this because in our consultations, we are paid $200 and are in the home on average for about 30 minutes. In another section, I'll be outlining our vacant staging consultation process, but for now, in an occupied staging job, we are in and out fast, which is why I'm ok with applying the fee to the full staging job once it's booked.

The second template I have is the BOOKING email; this is a generic confirmation email outlining the name of the stager, the address of the home, and the time of the appointment. This prevents any miscommunication when confirming these appointments. I've often been given an address from the listing realtor and when I entered it into the confirmation email going to the home owner, I had them reply, "By the way, our address is wrong here, it is actually XXXX". It's been an easy fail safe for my company when it comes to booking appointments.

Finally, the FOLLOW UP email; this is generally a courtesy email thanking them for their time and providing anything I promised them during the appointment, like formal quotes, info sheets, etc.

On page 97, I have provided a copy of what an SOP outline looks like for one of my booking templates. Here is a guideline of what should go into each email template for the service you provide.

Sales Email
- Greeting.
- Thank you for contacting us regarding our
  _____ (service).
- Your System: how do you perform your appointments (verbal, written, digital).
- Time Frame: how long will this appointment take?
- General overview of what you will be doing during this appointment.
- Fee for the appointment: if your fee depends on a variety of things, I like to give a range.
- Personal touch on how you look forward to helping them take on their project.
- Signature with contact information.
  - **Attachments:** we like to include for each sales email an "About us" PDF page that has a photo of our team, our DOM (days on market) stats, facts about our team, our USP (unique selling proposition, e.g.: we specialize in vacants), etc.

Booking Email
- Greeting.
- Thank you for booking a _____ (appointment type).
- You are confirmed for the following:
  - DATE

- • TIME
- • STAGER (this is if you have a team or it will be you)
- • CLIENT'S ADDRESS
- As mentioned in our previous email, this appointment consists of _____ (repeat from previous email, along with the time frame and what to expect).
- Should you have any questions, please do not hesitate to call.
- Signature with contact information.
    - **Attachments:** ALL of our appointments require a credit card form to be filled out, even if they choose to pay by cheque, as this is a precaution we've implemented for bounced cheques and to help us reduce the need to chase after people for payment.

Follow Up Email

- Greeting.
- Thank them for their time during the appointment.
- Relate to them personally & complement them on something from a nice home to a lovely family. This will help keep trust and relationship building.
- Provide them with any information you PROMISED. If you didn't promise them anything, use this email as a thank you for their time.

In the next pages, I provide a copy of the documents I created for each email template. This can also be pre-programmed into most CRM systems that allow for saved email templates. You will significantly improve your response time if you select the appropriate template, filling out only the necessary changes. Beyond that, I keep original documents stored in my Dropbox account.

Email Template – Appointment Confirmation – Agent pays

SOP – Appointment Confirmation with Home Owner & Real Estate Agent is paying the fee.

To: Home Owner
CC: Agent, Stager
BCC: CRM email to track discussions
Attachments: none

Hello

Thank you for booking a consultation with us. You are confirmed for the following:

Date:
Time:
Stager:
Client's Address:

All occupied homes start with an extremely detailed consultation where we use our exclusive "Home Evaluation Handbook" and execute our 6-step staging process to ensure each home's customized suggestions are perfect.

The consultation takes up to 2 hrs for the average home and we will cover the following:

-Curb Appeal Tips to attract buyers
-First impressions and how to increase the 'Wow factor'
-Traffic flow
-Lighting and window treatments
-Focal points
-Foundations and anchors in each room
-Highlighting any unique selling features
-ROI (Return on Investment) opportunities for you to take advantage of
-Creating an emotional connection to a specific buyer which

assists in our properties quickly transacting
-MUCH MORE!

This consultation is designed to provide you with ALL the answers you need for your home, so you can easily take the report and execute the suggestions room by room. But don't worry, we are a full service company. We can connect you to trades, furniture rentals, and we can provide you with quotes to make your job easier.

Should you have any questions, please do not hesitate to call.

Sincerely,

(Email End – With Pre-Programmed Signature)

The next templates I have on file are:
- Invitation to attend an event / tradeshow
  - Greeting
  - Want to get to know you
  - Outline of what they will learn / benefit
  - Prize draw – give something away
  - RSVP date & time
- Follow up email from meeting at a trade show or event
  - Greeting
  - We met at _____
  - Would love to meet over coffee & just chat
- Referral request email to home owner
  - Greeting
  - Thank them for recent business (optional)
  - Ask "Who do you know that needs our help"
  - Offer a referral incentive
- New realtor email
  - Greeting
  - Review of our consultation details
  - Pricing with an exclusive realtor discount based on volume when working with us (usually, buy 15 consults = 1 free)

- Fact sheet about us
- Asking who we can thank for referring them to us

YOUR OWN:
Company Email Templates

I am creating the 3-step email templates for the following services listed here:

1)	2)	3)
4)	5)	6)

Use the template outlines to create your own email templates for each service.

Email Template Service #1:
_____(service name)

Sales Template

Booking Template

Follow Up Template

Service Notes

Email Template Service #2:

_____(service name)

Sales Template

Booking Template

Follow Up Template

Service Notes

Email Template Service #3:

_____(service name)

Sales Template

Booking Template

Follow Up Template

Service Notes

Email Template Service #4:

_____(service name)

Sales Template

Booking Template

Follow Up Template

Service Notes

Email Template Service #5:

_____(service name)

Sales Template

Booking Template

Follow Up Template

Service Notes

Email Template Service #6:

_____(service name)

Sales Template

Booking Template

Follow Up Template

Service Notes

Company Email Signature Template (all staff to use template)

Name: _____

Position: _____

Phone Number: _____

Email: _____

Webpage: _____

Logo: _____

Congratulations! Your core communication systems are now all set! You have established how you are going to operate, which services you are going to provide, and what communications templates you will use for each service so you can follow up accordingly. Now it's time to talk about necessary paperwork that goes along with each job. I will be providing you with some examples and copies of my templates for systems I've been using in my home staging business. The two that I am going to focus on here are contracts and credit card processing.

Kristy Morrison

Contracts Overview

This will be the hardest topic of them all because rules will vary from state to state and province to province. Here, I will be outlining general terms you'll want to discuss with your lawyers, to have them incorporated into your agreement so you and your clients are protected accordingly. All contracts are signed by the clients and kept in the main office for safe keeping in a locked filing cabinet. All records are also required to be kept for seven years. *(Your timeline will be outlined in the employment guidelines for your area.)*

LEGAL COVERAGE ASSISTANCE

Before we get into the actual contracts for our staging businesses, I need to share that I fully believe in using professionals to do what they do best. YES, lawyers can be expensive, but there are options available to us, you just have to be open to learning about them.

I have a contract where I pay $25/month and I get business lawyers on call through a legal broker. They can review contracts and even write up contracts at discounted rates.

This legal coverage plan is brokered through a direct sales (network marketing) company, and like most direct sales companies, they don't waste money on marketing which is how they can offer great pricing. I personally love these proven companies and business models that have been around for years and offer people savings by not having costly marketing expenses. Some will claim they are "scams" or "pyramid schemes", but with some proper research on the industry, you'll learn that a company that has been around longer than 5 years is 100% not a scam; our Canadian & American governments wouldn't allow something like that to last that long. Like the case is for all companies, you'll find positive and negative reviews of whatever you research. If you SEARCH for negative reviews, you'll find them, if you SEARCH for positive reviews, you'll find them too. Be smart and use reputable sources for making an informed decision, because the opinion of "Joe Blow from Tim-Buck-Two" shouldn't mean anything to you. If you're a serious business owner that knows how to do proper research, you'll look at the Direct Selling Association, the Better Business Bureau, third-party reviews in magazines, etc.

Now, as a side note so that I am clear: I am not a representative for this specific business nor do I have any affiliations with them. I am not paid to promote this business either, I am just a happy customer with their legal program. For the representative's contact information to see how you could yourself become a customer or to get more details on what they offer, see the resources section of this book.

My legal services currently include the following:
subject to change by provider
- Legal Consultation & Assistance Services
- Unlimited review of personal legal documents of 10 pages or less
- Will Benefits
- Power of Attorney for Property
- Power of Attorney for Personal Care
- Warranty Issues
- Lease Agreements
- Government Agencies
- Debt Collection
- Tenant Legal Advice
- Small Claims Court
- Consumer Protection Assistance
- Social Assistance Legal Advice
- Estate Settlement Advice
- All other legal work at a 25% discount off the providing law firm's hourly rate
- & Much More.

Contracts Checklist

Now back to our contracts. Here is a checklist of all the contracts I believe you should have written up for your staging business:

- Occupied Home Contract Generated
- Vacant Staging Contract Generated
- Credit Card Forms Generated (see explanation and template in the next chapter)
- Non-Disclosure / Non-Compete Agreement Generated
- Other Service Agreement Generated:_____
- Other Service Agreement Generated:_____
- Other Service Agreement Generated:_____
- Other Service Agreement Generated:_____
- Other Service Agreement Generated:_____
- Other Service Agreement Generated:_____

Occupied Home Contract
- Agreement between the home owner & the company.
- Warranties of our work; in our industry we cannot guarantee homes will sell immediately because we are only a piece of the puzzle, the realtor / marketing are huge factors too.
- Terms regarding being indemnified from any form of potential lawsuits.
- Payment Terms
    - Payment upon completion of the consultation.
    - Payment is provided by the realtor and the home owner owes us nothing.
- Photography clause allowing us to take photos as we walk through the home and we do not owe the home owner any royalty fees for the use of photos in marketing materials.
- Space for "TESTIMONIALS" on our agreement forms so we can get feedback.
- Client Signatures.

Vacant Staging Contract
- Agreement between the home owner & the company.
- Address of service to be performed.
- Address of billing & of mailing, if different.

Capital Home
Staging & Design

Capital Home Staging & Design Home Owner Account

Date:_____

Please fill out this form and send back to us BEFORE your first appointment with us.

Name:_____

Office:_____

Office Address:_____

_____, Ontario, _____

Billing Address of the CREDIT CARD:_____

_____, Ontario, _____

All Vacant Staging's require an account set up with a valid credit card on file for incidentals.

- ✓ Home Staging Consultations
- ✓ Vacant Consultations
- ✓ Inventory Rental
- ✓ Colour Consultations
- ✓ Staging To Live
- ✓ FREE Consultations for MILITARY FAMILIES**

**Note Owner must pay the regular consultation fee and claim it through the government. Visit our webpage for more information.

Scan & Email to:
info@chsd.ca

Email:_____

Phone:_____ Cell_____

Preference of Payment:
☐ Credit Card ☐ Cash –delivery ☐ Interact Email ☐ Check
Note: Credit Cards will be processed upon completion of the job.

Credit card: (as seen on card) ☐Visa ☐MC

Name:_____

Number:_____

Expiry:_____ CCID_____

Signature:_____
(By: Signing you authorize Capital Home Staging & Design to automatically process your card the day of if selected above OR on the 30th day if alternate payment has not been received.)

Note: We cannot accept AMEX cards at this time

Would you like to receive our Newsletter? ☐YES ☐NO

Would you like us to advise you when we are hosting a Home Staging Training Event and require properties to stage at significantly discounted prices? ☐YES ☐NO

Notes for account:_____

_____

_____

Who can we thank for your business?_____

_____

Who do you know that may need our help?_____

_____

Capital Home Staging & Design
613-832-8958 | info@chsd.ca
www.CapitalHomeStagingAndDesign.ca

- Client's contact information.
- Outline of services being provided & cost.

- Disclaimer of warranties; we will do our best, however, due to many factors, we cannot guarantee their home will sell in a timely manner.
- Photo & Marketing Terms
    - Owners allow company to take photos to use in future marketing.
    - Owner is not entitled to financial compensation.
    - The company is the owner of the photos.
- Payment Terms
    - Vacant jobs require payment in full upfront.
    - No cancellation of staging once the staging process has started, unless the contracts have been signed within the last 7 days, the client will get a 50% refund, if signed within 24hrs, the client will get a 75% refund and we will keep 25% for our administration fees.
- Unlisted service fees based on variables.
    - Unplowed laneway restricting access to the home prior to staging will result in $500 rescheduling fee.
    - Cancellation or rescheduling of job in less than 24hrs will result in a $500 rescheduling fee.
    - Any fees from condo corporations for elevator usage will be passed onto the client.
    - Home renovations still in process & not complete with a thorough & professional cleaning will result in a $500 rescheduling fee.
- Governing law and location of where the contract is valid and bound.
    - Client Signatures.
    - Staff Signatures.

Employee Confidentiality, Non-Disclosure and Non-Solicitation Agreement

WHEREAS Capital Home Staging & Design (the Company) desires to engage **Tania Wojciechowski** (the Employee) to provide services to the Company as the **Professional Staging Assistant**, and the Employee agrees to provide such services, all in consideration and upon the terms and conditions contained in this Agreement, the parties agree as follows:

Confidentiality and Non-Disclosure

1. The Employee acknowledges that, during the course of her/his employment, the Employee may acquire confidential information, which includes without limitation:

    a. intellectual property, including trademarks and trademark applications, trade names, trade secrets, certification marks, patents and patent applications, copyrights, know-how, formulae, processes, inventions, technical expertise, research data, industrial designs, registrations and applications for registration, patterns, discoveries, devices and compilations of information;

    b. technical information, including methods, compositions, systems, techniques, machines, computer programs and research projects;

    c. business information, including customer lists and information, referral sources, business plans, business opportunities, pricing data, sources of supply, financial data and marketing, forecasts, production data, and merchandising information, systems or plans; and

    d. work product resulting from or relating to work performed by the Employee.

2. The Employee agrees that she/he shall not, except with the prior written consent of the Company, at any time during or following the term of the Employee's employment, directly or indirectly disclose, divulge, reveal, report, publish, transfer or use for any purpose any of the confidential information that has been acquired by the Employee as a result of her/his employment with the Company.

3. The Employee agrees that, during her/his employment and thereafter, all confidential information is and shall remain the property of the Company. Upon the Employee's termination, or at any time the Company may request, the Employee shall immediately return to the Company all copies of any confidential information in the Employee's possession or control. The Employee shall not retain copies, notes or abstracts of the confidential information.

Capital Home Staging & Design
5450 Canotek Rd, Suite 68, Ottawa, On K1J9G5
(613) 832-8958 | info@chsd.ca | www.CapitalHomeStagingAndDesign.ca

Page 1
Bird Anderson

114

Non-Solicitation

4. The Employee acknowledges that she/he will gain knowledge of and have a close relationship with the Company's employees, customers and clients, which would injure the Company if made available to a competitor or used for competitive purposes. The Employee agrees that, during the term of her/his employment, and for a period of six months following the termination of employment for any reason, the Employee will not, directly or indirectly, in any manner whatsoever:

   a. hire or take away, or facilitate, assist, cause to be hired or taken away, any employee of the Company for the purposes of employment in any business related to or competitive with the business of the Company; or

   b. approach, solicit, accept business or employment with, service, or otherwise deal with any customer or client of the Company in order to attempt to direct any such customer or client away from the Company.

5. For the purposes of paragraph 4, the parties agree that the definition of "customer or client" includes anyone, such as an agent or home owner, with whom the Employee has had dealings by virtue of the employment relationship within the preceding six months.

Recognition

6. The Employee recognizes that:

   a. in the event that any provision or part of this Agreement is deemed invalid by a court of competent jurisdiction, the remaining provisions or parts shall remain in full force and effect;

   b. the covenants contained in this Agreement are necessary for the protection of the Company's legitimate business interests and are reasonable in scope and content; and

   c. a breach of any of the foregoing provisions will give rise to irreparable harm and injury non-compensable in damages. Accordingly, the Company or such other party may seek and obtain injunctive relief against the breach or threatened breach of the foregoing provisions, in addition to any other legal remedies that may be available. The Employee agrees that an injunction will not prevent her/him from earning a reasonable livelihood.

Survival

7. This Agreement shall survive the termination of the employment relationship for any reason and shall be enforceable notwithstanding the existence of any claim or cause of action of the Employee against the Company, whether predicated upon this Agreement or otherwise.

Capital Home Staging & Design
5450 Canotek Rd, Suite 68. Ottawa, On K1J9G5
(613) 832-8958 | info@chsd.ca | www.CapitalHomeStagingAndDesign.ca

Page 2
Bird Anderson

115

Non-Disclosure / Non-Compete Agreements

This is something I wanted for my business from the start. I chose to have staff, and I really wanted to have a unique business system that was ours and that no one else could duplicate. It is true that most NDA (Non-Disclosure Agreements) don't hold up in court, however, each state and province does allow them to be valid for a specific timeframe. In Ontario, it is for a maximum of 6 months, longer than that and you'll be hard-pressed to find a judge who will let it fly.

You will want to hire a local lawyer to draft up your own copy of an NDA so it's legal and applicable in your area. Next is a screen shot of the NDA for my staff in Ottawa, drafted by an employment lawyer for us based on our company goals and terms. This will not be suitable for everyone, as each NDA needs to be customized to your end goal desires for your business and how you want past staff to be treated and restricted by.

One thing I learned in my years of hiring is that any potential staff member who DOESN'T want to sign an NDA will not be hired in my company, because to me it's a clear indication they are just wanting to work with us to become a direct competitor later on. This has saved me plenty of heartaches when it comes to hiring, firing and dealing with shady past staff that try and sneak one under the radar by using our systems or property when they open up their own business, even years down the road.

You will want to outline the following:
- Agreement between the employee & the company.
- List of confidential information they may obtain & must remain private.
    - i.e.: Systems, Processes, Trademarks, Patents, Inventions, Materials, etc.
- Agreement that employee will not directly or indirectly share information.
- Agreement that employee will not poach staff or customers.

- What is a customer and who is exempt.
- Breach of contract will result in what repercussions.

Kristy Morrison

Credit Card Processing

If you are a business and you do not accept credit cards, then you are shooting yourself in the foot. EVERY business should have the capability of processing the most preferred method of payment.

FACTS

✓ Did you know that 4 out of 5 people prefer using plastic (debit or credit) over cash?

✓ Mobile wallets (where you pay directly with your phone through an app from your bank) are the future of merchant processing.

✓ Accepting credit cards can increase business as much as 23%.

✓ Improved cash flow with immediate payments; cheques can clear in 15-90 days depending on the amount of the transaction.

✓ Customers paying with a credit card typically spend 20% more than if they were paying with cash.

✓ Lower operational costs and customer tracking with the simple processing of credit cards, resulting in overall increased profit margins in your business.

✓ Enhance your business image; by accepting credit cards, you gain credibility with potential customers, showing that you are a true business and have all the necessary tools to get a job done.

✓ In 2006, Visa and MasterCard together participated in approximately 94% of the value of credit card transactions in Canada, with a 64% and 30% share respectively.[1]

✓ The US credit card market is also highly concentrated: Visa and MasterCard accounted for approximately 75% of the market value in 2008.[2] Eight years later, credit card processing is closer to the 90% range of preferred usage.

---

[1] http://www.parl.gc.ca/content/lop/researchpublications/prb0910-e.htm

[2] Idem.

Now that you have the facts all laid out and you agree having the ability to process credit cards is a valuable tool to have in your business, you'll want to find the RIGHT processing system for you. Personally, I've tried a few online and cell phone systems from PayPal to Square, and though they did the job of processing cards and dumping the money into my account, I found their customer service hard to deal with when I had a processing issue. Also, their processing fees looked great at first because they had no monthly fees, however as my business grew, the more money I processed, the more I spent on those fees. After years of searching for another solution, I was called up by one of my realtor clients (shout out to Wendy Cheung & Craig Barton Hill), and it went a little something like this...

Wendy: "Hey Kristy, it's Wendy. Listen, I got a question for ya... How would you like to save on your credit card processing fees?"

Me: "Uhhhh, who the heck wouldn't want to save??"

Wendy: (laughing) "That's what I thought! So I'm going to submit your name for a free analysis with Anovia Payments and one of their reps will get back to you within 24hrs to obtain a copy of your current processing statement. Then, they will provide you with a clear black and white comparison of what fees you're paying with your current provider and what fees you would be paying if you were using Anovia."

Me: "Sure, sounds good... Thanks Wendy."

(As a side note, I was kind of like, CRAP... now that I'm being quoted and Wendy is a client, if I don't want to change providers, I might jeopardize our relationship! Fear began brewing in my belly...)

Long story short, even though I was scared of losing a client, I submitted my current processing statement with PayPal, just to see what the numbers would be like. Much to my surprise, the quote came back with savings of about $1,000.00 in 1 year if I was using Anovia instead of PayPal. WOW!!! $1,000.00 was FOUND in my business, that's amazing! And the best part is I learned that with every year of growth in my business, the savings would increase because they didn't have any of the hidden rates most processing companies have.

So I signed the paperwork and started using Anovia Payments. Like with anything, there is a learning curve when using a new system; for example, knowing how to process funds and figuring out the easiest way to enter things in the terminal, but with a little effort and training, I was hooked. I was so glad Wendy & Craig approached me for these savings. I have actually found that most of our fears come from the unknown, and that's why most people don't take action. However, if I had let fear run my business, I wouldn't have found the savings I'm enjoying right now with many of my business services.

Quick Case Study

We all know the fabulous Lori Kim Polk out of California. She identified that she was using Square to process her customers credit cards. Since Anovia guarantee's savings she had nothing to lose with a quote.

Anovia found: $300.00 a month in processing fee's saved! That's $3,600.00 a year. Best part is as she grows the more she saves.

Now, not everyone does the same volume of work Lori and I do, so many will be asking *"Why should I pay $15-30 in monthly fees when I don't have a consistent volume of work?"* Well, you'll need to establish how important a few things are to you and your company. Is the high-level of security worth it to you and your clients over "group processing systems" that operate on a batch system and lump payments? Do you want to go through the hassle of setting up and learning how to use a "free" monthly account with high processing fees or learn a superior system from day one, avoiding the hassle of change later? I know if I had had access to Anovia seven years ago, I would've been glad to start using it from day one, because implementing a new system when we were busy wasn't easy. It was totally worth it, but not as easy as starting with it directly with the launch of my business. For myself, time is money and I want to be efficient at all times. Also, you have to remember these monthly service fees are a company write-off.

Clear Benefits of Anovia
✓ Collective buying power for savings to business owners.
✓ Competitive Rates – They will meet or beat your current total processing cost, or they will give you $100 Visa gift card!!!
✓ State-of-the-Art Products – Anovia offers a broad range of products from online processing, mobile solutions, and handheld devices.
✓ Secure and Reliable Technology – Anovia uses a proven processing platform, handling more than 1 billion dollars in transactions annually.
✓ Transparent Fees – No more surprises with downgraded penalties or unexpected fees.

HOT TIP: Anovia guarantees savings to business owners who process, on average, over $3,000 a month, and if they can't beat their current rate, the business owner will get a $100 Visa gift card for their time. *(This offer may change at any time.)*

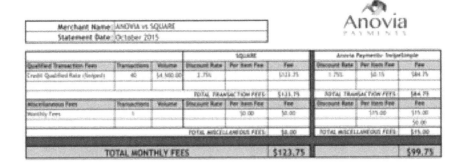

Here is an example comparison of a hypothetical account that is processing $4,500 in monthly billing. You can see that this customer would have an estimated annual savings of $288.00, which is an effective cost reduction of nearly 20%.

Just think of what you can do when you position yourself for savings and future growth.

Processing Made Easy

We have evaluated our processing needs and established ourselves with a company that can grow with us as we grow, we'll now want to implement a system on how to get paid EASILY! In my experience, whenever I allowed realtors or home owners to pay us by cash or cheque, it took nearly 30, 60, 90 and even 120 days to collect the money because they "kept forgetting" to pay us.

On the next page is a copy of the merchant processing form we use for our home owner and realtor clients. (Note: We can accept AMEX processing, I just choose not to personally accept it because AMEX's processing fees are much higher.)

Why Is Cash Flow Important?

Guest Author: James Fellows of Finanscapes.
See resources page for more info & a coupon for cash flow forecasting charts.

The number one cause of businesses failing is CASH FLOW ISSUES! Put simply, cash flow is the cash coming into and going out of your business at any given time. But why is this so important? It may sound like an obvious question, but you would be surprised at the number of start-ups we hear about who think that profit and cash flow are the same thing – they aren't!

At the end of each month or at the end of your financial year, you will know if you have made more money than you have spent, but what about on a day-to-day basis? Good fiscal management means always having a surplus of cash within the business to cover unforeseen expenses and disasters, and help you take advantage of unexpected opportunities. Whereas with a negative cash flow (i.e. no surplus cash within the business), you will quickly run into problems, including paying bills, staff and suppliers, and not being able to invest in the business through marketing or technology. This is why understanding your cash flow is crucial.

What Is A Cash Flow Forecast?

A regularly updated and reviewed cash flow forecast can make the difference between success and failure for many businesses, not just start-ups. A cash flow forecast is a forward-looking view of the incoming and outgoing cash of your business each month, over a fixed period of time – normally a year. The simplest way of seeing what your cash flow will look like is in a graph.

FINANSCAPES has built a simple dashboard into their cash flow forecasting tool to ensure it is as simple and easy to interpret as possible. Your cash flow forecast will indicate when you are going to experience positive and negative cash flow, giving you the opportunity to put precautionary measures in place now to avert any crisis. Your forecast will also give you an idea of the amount of cash you are likely to have available at any particular time, indicating possible windows for growth and investment. This will help you make plans for the future.

How to Calculate Your Cash Flow

We have written an extensive article, "How to Calculate Cash Flow"[3], which explains what numbers you will need to have on hand and how to use them to calculate an accurate cash flow. We have created a simple 4-step process for calculating it, that way you can understand the numbers in your cash flow forecast.

Once you have these numbers and you know how to calculate a basic cash flow for the present, you can start using a forecasting tool such as ours to predict your cash flow into the future.

The Advantages of Having a Cash Flow Forecast

By now, I'm sure you have realized there are almost endless possibilities once you have a cash flow forecast in hand.

It allows you to:
- See your options clearly and at a quick glance.
- Make better decisions based on the figures and not a hunch.
- Remove the risks from decision making and business strategizing.
- Make growth plans.
- Improve relationships with suppliers, staff and customers.
- Dedicate more time to other (more fun) tasks.
- Foresee problems before they happen, giving you the chance to correct them before it costs money!

- Build your investor confidence.

The FINANSCAPES forecasting tool allows you to calculate both your cash flow and profit vs loss, increasing your chances of start-up success. You can compare scenarios and plans to see which ones will be most profitable and leave you with the best cash flow.

And what if you need funding for your idea or start-up? Forecasting is an essential part of any loan or financing application and with the publishing functionality FINANSCAPES offers, you will have a professional-looking forecast to show bank managers, mentors or investors at the touch of a button.

CRM Systems and Getting Set Up

CRM (Client Relationship Management) systems are needed to track jobs, wins, losses, emails received, notes made about certain clients or jobs, and so much more. CRM systems are so specific to each business needs that I cannot definitely select one for you and say "go use this one" because I don't know your business goals or requirements. However, I will provide you with a few suggestions of current online systems that you can research and evaluate for your own needs.

17 HATS

This is the only time I'm going to recommend something that I don't personally use and it's not because I don't want to, but because I've spent so much time customizing our current system and we are so far invested that it's not feasible for me to make the jump. So if you are starting out or want a wicked system, you'll want to check out 17 Hats' CRM Systems.

With 17 Hats, you can:

- Get an overview of your business.
- Track all your contacts in one place.
- Manage multiple projects at once.
- Create custom questionnaires for clients.
- Build and send out quotes.
- Have clients sign contracts online.
- Keep track of accounts and do your bookkeeping.
- Track your time and invoice clients.
- Sync your email accounts.
- Create to-do lists and reminders.
- Use their WorkFlow program.
- Capture leads with specific tools.

Here are some other CRM systems that you can evaluate and see what suits your needs and budgets the best. I strongly suggest ones that have GOOGLE calendar integration.

-**insightly.com** – *I personally use this one and I'm too far committed to make a change at this point.*
-**contactually.com**
-**zoho.com**
-**highrise.com**
-**17Hats.com** – *Very robust and allows for automation.*
-**infustionsoft.com** – *This one is a BEAST and is very expensive, but you can do everything you ever desired.*

Now that you have your CRM selected, you'll want to get it all set up. YES, it's going to take time, but Rome wasn't built in a day! If you are busy, then you will have to block time yourself and schedule it in. The most common complaint I hear from stagers is, "I don't have the time". While it may be true that running a business, taking care of family, attending social events, and so much more, take up a lot of time, we all have but 24hrs in a day. If Sir Richard Branson can run multiple empires, why can't you? He doesn't have a magical 100hr-day, he has the same 24hrs we all have. He has just used the proven method of leverage in his business ventures, and if you are truly that busy, you'll want to consider hiring. If you can't afford to hire an assistant, you'll need to carefully evaluate your priorities and if you spend most of your time doing activities that don't generate an income for the business, then maybe running a business is not the best avenue for you.

I don't mean to be harsh, but to run a true company that is sellable, you need to be profitable, and buyers generally look for self-sufficient companies that do not require them to do 100% of the work. They want to buy a business, not a job. Bottom line, we are all busy; if you can't do it, hire an assistant (we'll outline this later on in the book).

GOOGLE CALENDAR

I am a major fan of Google Calendar (G-Cal). I've been using it in my business since day one, and it has enabled me to keep up with our needs and growing team. To start using G-Cal and checking Mail, go to www.Google.com and click on "Login" in the top right corner of the page where you will enter your email account & password. Watch the following YouTube videos to see a complete tutorial on how to use G-Cal on your computer:

Mac: http://www.youtube.com/watch?v=2woEQUpMQcY
MS 2011: http://www.youtube.com/watch?v=M68_Si1icq4

Needed Calendars

First, you'll want to set up an office/company email address, this will be your primary calendar. You'll also want to set up an account for each employee and yourself so everyone can have their own calendars to play around with.

Here's a list of the calendars, I created for my own business needs:

1. Main office
    i. Shared with everyone on the team and detailing days closed, team holidays, staff meetings, events, etc.
2. Owner of the company
    i. Eventually as you delegate, you won't want the team to know your every move.
3. Team members
    i. Each team member should have their own G-Cal, this way they can see ONLY their appointments booked & the main office calendar.

You can see above the following calendars with appointments listed:

-Main office – Pink
-Owner Kristy – Purple
-Stager Patricia – Blue
-Stager Tania – Yellow
-Stager Mandy – Orange

Each team member can ONLY see their scheduled appointments to reduce confusion, but the main office can see them ALL. This is set up in the settings section of your G-Cal, as well as who you authorize to see which specific appointments.

G-Cal also has the option of syncing your schedule with your smart phone. This will allow staff to check emails and have their schedule at hand so appointments are not missed. To get a tutorial on how to do this, check out these YouTube videos:

iPhones: http://www.youtube.com/watch?v=zPM73Qas21I
Android: http://www.yourtube.com/watch?v=gC9Uvh3NngA

When I am creating the team's G-Cals, I have a set system on the names and passwords we use so it's easier to help my staff when a login issue happens. Every account has specific email titles, such as:

Office: Chsd.office@gmail.com
Staff: Chsd.staff2@gmail.com
            Chsd.staff3@gmail.com
            Chsd.staff4@gmail.com

This way, if a teammate leaves, I can give their account to the next employee without having to create a new one all over again with a specific name, like Samantha@gmail.com becoming Jordan@gmail.com. Also, when the email account stays general like shown above, if a client isn't aware that Samantha has left and her email address is no longer valid, the client's email will still reach an employee who can take over the client's account or do a follow up on the client's needs. On top of that, all of the passwords are set up sequentially and the staff don't know each other's passwords. I save them in an Excel document on my computer in Dropbox. E.g.: Password1 becomes Password2 when the employee leaves, and then becomes Password3 when that employee leaves, etc.

Setting Up Your Own Accounts

Office: _____@gmail.com
      Password: _____
      Access to: _____

Owner: _____@gmail.com
      Password: _____
      Access to: Office & _____

Staff #1: _____@gmail.com
      Password: _____
      Access to: Office & _____

Staff #2: _____@gmail.com
    Password: _____
    Access to: Office & _____

Staff #3: _____@gmail.com
    Password: _____
    Access to: Office & _____

Staff #4: _____@gmail.com
    Password: _____
    Access to: Office & _____

Staff #5: _____@gmail.com
    Password: _____
    Access to: Office & _____

Staff #6: _____@gmail.com
    Password: _____
    Access to: Office & _____

Movers: _____@gmail.com
    Password: _____
    Access to: Office & _____

Required Dates for Calendar (Time Blocking)

Once your calendars are created and ready to be used, the first thing you'll want to do is plan your year in advance as much as you possibly can. If you are able to schedule things in an automatic rotation, it will make life so much easier.

- Birthdays of loved ones you will need time for. (E.g.: spouse, kids, parents, yours, etc.)
- Industry-Related Events
    - RESA Convention (every January, generally 3rd week)
    - IDS Furniture Show (January – Toronto)
    - Highpoint Furniture Market (April & September)
    - Vegas Furniture Market (January & July/August)

- Staff Events
    - Summer BBQ
    - Christmas Dinner
- Staff Meetings (E.g.: Every 2nd Saturday of the month from 9am to 12pm.)
- Local Trade Shows
    - Local Real Estate Board
    - Home Shows
    - Renovation Shows
- Vacations
    - Since this is flexible, I always schedule "month" times. (I.e.: In February / March, I will take a 2-week vacation. In August, I will take a 1 week vacation at the cottage.)

Those are typically the bulky elements we encounter in our lives. Even if you do not plan on attending these shows, I still write them in their respective months because sometimes, after there is a local home show, business picks up so it allows me to track how busy we are in relation to the local home and renovation shows.

Next, because I have a team, I have SET times when we book our consultations so as to increase efficiency of booking. Too often, we were getting calls of, "Can you meet me at 11am?", and that's smack dab in the middle of the morning, ultimately canceling out any possibility of a previous appointment. For every time we have the inability to book a consultation, it's lost income for the business, which is why we changed to having a set time schedule for our appointments. Each of our consultations are 2hrs long, so I know that if I book a 9am appointment, I will be done at 11am and will be able to get to my next appointment with enough travel time for 12pm.

Here's our set time schedule for appointments:

Monday – Friday
9:00am, 12:00pm, 3:00pm and 6:00pm.

Saturday
9:00am, 12:00pm and 3:00pm.

Sunday
Closed

Time Blocking Technique

This tool is the single most beneficial element that I use in my life to be at my MAXIMUM efficiency. The best book to truly learn and train on this system is called, *"No B.S. Time Management for Entrepreneurs" by Dan Kennedy*.

Essentially, I make a list of things I HAVE to accomplish in my business often, and only AFTER I create that core schedule of things to complete will I book staging appointments or realtor meetings or any other tasks.

1) Social Media – blog content, tweets, fact posts, stat-boosting images, etc.
2) Thank You letters to realtor and builder clients.
3) Accounting & Invoicing / Payroll (I outsource, but many of you will have to add this to your list.)
4) Writing Sessions – newsletters, articles, books, etc.
5) Personal Development – reading books, attending courses…

At first, I try and pack it all into one day for "office efficiency", like Tuesdays / Wednesdays are the slowest days for me, so I book my time in a similar manner:

- 8-11am – Research & compile social media content. Also turn them into photos using **canva.com**. I try and get as many photo posts done as possible during this time.
- 11-12pm – Thank You letters to past realtor and builder clients.
- 12-12:30pm – Lunch Break.
- 12:30-2pm – Accounting & Invoicing / Payroll.
- 2-5pm – Writing session.

- 5-6pm – Personal Development (every day!)

This works best for me, but some of you will get greater benefit from time blocking per day. I.e.: Writing sessions every day from 8-9am, Thank You letters every Thursday at 5pm, etc. Only you can decide how to set your time, but the KEY to success is putting it in your calendar and STICKING TO IT no matter what. Too busy to do any office work? Like I mentioned before, you clearly need to hire administrative help.

BONUS: 12-FOLDER SYSTEM

This system is perfect to get a fail-safe system for vacant properties. Often we put renewals into our G-Cal, however, sometimes mistakes are made and something is overlooked. Missing a renewal can be a very costly mistake, especially when working with third-party inventory rental companies, because they don't care if you forgot to charge the client, they run a business and you'll get charged yourself.

To ensure renewals or meetings are not missed, we have a 12-folder system. You will need the following items to implement this system:
- Labels & markers
- 1 hanging folder box
- 12 hanging folders, labeled January – December
- 8 manila folders, labeled Week 1-4 (you will make two sets of Week 1-4)

How it works:
- Use one set of Week 1-4 manila folders and put them in the hanging folder of the current month you are in. The next set of Week 1-4 manila folders will be placed in the hanging folder of the following month.
  - E.g.: Today is January 1st, so January's hanging folder will have your first set of Week 1-4 manila folders and the next set of Week 1-4 will go in the month of February folder.

- All important documents are filed away in your hanging folder box. During each month, you take a look at each weekly folder and deal with the tasks outlined in that folder of the week.
  - E.g.: A vacant staging is set up for week 4 of January, you file away the paperwork with that information in the Week 4 manila folder in January's hanging folder, so once you get to that week, you are reminded to deal with this task.
  - E.g.: A vacant staging renewal is due February 25? File away that document in Week 4 of the February folder.
- As you finish the week's tasks, you place that weekly folder in the next empty month's hanging folder. Your weekly folders are always being rotated from month to month.
  - E.g.: January's Week 2 is done and all tasks have been completed. The Week 2 folder is now placed in the March folder behind Week 1.
- As future tasks come up, put a reminder document in the appropriate month folder of when you want to complete it. Once your weekly folders are up in that rotation, file away the reminder in the best weekly folder for the completion of the task.
  - E.g.: An event is coming up in October and you're still in January? File away the task in the month of August so you are reminded to apply and be ready for it in October. Once the weekly folders are placed in the month of August, decide during which week you'll want to have accomplished the task and file away the reminder in that week's folder.

Setting Up Fieldwork Systems & Inventory Tracking

Fieldwork SOPs

This is where the fun starts to happen! Well, it's only fun when you don't feel like a chicken with their head cut off running around in circles. Systems come into play at this point; if we can systemize the fieldwork so that you and everyone on your team can be efficient and productive, your profit margins will increase. I'll focus on the 2 primary services of being a home stager: the occupied home and the vacant staging appointments, from consultations and beyond.

Occupied Home Consultations

First, you'll want to establish how you are going to perform your consultations. Verbal walk & talks? Digital recordings? Written reports? Emailed reports? There are many ways to perform a staging consultation and honestly, there is no right or wrong way, just what works best for you.

I chose to use the written report and compiled a 57 page consultation book that outlines every room in the home and lists many generic checklist items that we encounter often, like dust baseboards, keep toilet seats down, touch up wall damage, change light switch covers if they are anything but white, etc.

Beyond the generic checklists, each section has enough space to write suggestions as far as other things we want to improve on, from addressing outdated elements to items that are missing and how the staging should take place.

Here is a list of what is covered in our consultation books:
- Introduction to the home owner
- Summary of our recommendations (1 page)
- Entrance
- Bathrooms – with space for 3 bathrooms
- Living Room & Family Room – with layout section
- Dining Room – with layout section
- Kitchen
- Stairways & Hallways
- Bedrooms – with space for 4 bedrooms and layout section
- Loft spaces & Home offices
- Laundry Rooms
- Basements – with layout section
- Additional Notes – for extra space to write
- Exit Letter & Stager's Contact Info
- Discount coupon of 15-50% – for repeat business, to be used on the next house, not applicable to showcasing jobs

When you find an avenue that works, stick to it. If you hire team members and they are really good at a fast walk and talk session, then you can consider expanding on your services' list, but not until you have a firm system that works for YOU in the first place.

I was trained by Karen Schaefer, founder of APSD (Association of Property Scene Designers), on their exclusive "Staging Pyramid for Success". Not only I, but ALL of my staff are trained through APSD, so our systems are the same throughout our staging process and company growth. Unfortunately, because she is the owner of those systems and training courses, I cannot give you my full staging process. However, here is a copy of the 3 sets of goals to achieve during our Home Staging Consultations.

---

3 Sets of Goals - Home Staging

Prior to Consulting on the Property

1) Secure information on the seller & the property history. Use the Staging Project Sheet.
      i.   Admin is to obtain as much information as possible.
      ii. Stager is to fill out the Staging Project Sheet by questioning home owners.
2) Receive a signed contract with staging terms, expectations, and payment.
      i.   Contract is with whomever is paying.
      ii. Have a separate photographer waver for home owners if the payment is coming from the Realtor.
3) Familiarize yourself with the sales & marketing history (actual vs. what you have been told)

During The Staging Consultation

1) Have a full and complete understanding of the seller's goals (time frame, pricing, wishes etc.)
2) Follow the APSD (Association of Property Scene Designers) Pyramid for success.
3) Get a testimonial BEFORE you leave (primarily on vacant + showcased properties)
      i.   Testimonials page.
4) Offer your up-sell -Cleaning, landscaping, photography all outsourced parters offer a 10% referral fee.

After The Staging Consultation

1) Send a "Thank you" cards via -snail mail.

2) Follow up o the sale of the property -price & days on market until contracted.
3) Up-Sell if it didn't happen - email / letter / call
4) Request additional bookings - at least one referral.
   i. For agents "How many other houses do you have that you think I can help with?"

In my company, we choose NOT to rent out accessories to our occupied home clients because, from previous experiences, they always came back dirty or damaged, and even went missing. Also, dealing with clients on the level of, "Where is my green pillow?" with the response of, "Well, I don't know, but I paid you a rental fee for 3 months this winter, so I'm sure I paid for the value of the missing pillow." You can either fight it and irritate a client, or absorb the lost cost and move on, hoping to keep the clients on good terms and obtain referral jobs. Another reason we choose not to rent out our own inventory to occupied homes is for sanitary reasons. Dust, allergens, smoke and mites, among other things, are a necessary part of living and EVERY home has them.

FACTS
* It's estimated that the average bed has over 10,000 house dust mites living in it, which will result in there being over two million droppings. Times this by the number of beds found in a home (usually from 2-5)... YUCK!
* House dust mites are just as comfortable living in the sofa, soft cushions and carpets.
* In the USA, as many as 3/10 people who have allergies are allergic to pet dander.
* Bed bugs can live ANYWHERE. Pest professionals have treated infestations 89% of the time in the common home (vs hotel), 88% in condos, 67% in hotels, 35% in college dorms, 4% in movie theatres.
* Bed bugs are hardy; these pests can live for several months without a blood meal. This means they can linger in furniture, bags and suitcases for a long time until they are near a human host again. In addition, bed bugs can survive temperatures of nearly freezing to 122 degrees. Because of this, bed bugs are

not a pest that can be treated with DIY measures. Professional pest control is the most effective way to treat an infestation.[4]

* Bed bugs are smart; they know to stay out of view during the daytime, hiding in crevices and box springs, baseboards, behind wallpaper. When we go to sleep, they are alerted of our presence with the carbon dioxide that we exhale as we breathe.

As you can see, even just a few facts were enough to make me close up my warehouse and reduce contamination. Could you imagine what would happen if our staging warehouse became contaminated with bed bugs or a ton of allergens? NO THANK YOU!

When talking to clients of occupied homes (DURING the job, not before), we generally say the following:

"Now, to finish your home staging process, I've provided a list of areas we need to improve on for your visual WOW factor. Since this is a lived-in home, I'm sure you can appreciate that we do not rent out our items for sanitary reasons. We don't want to have items transferred from home to home and cause a potential contamination of allergies or pests. But, we will be happy to do a ½ day shopping package to get you specifically all the items that you'll need to finish off your home properly."

Usually, that has a positive response from home owners going, "Ohhh! I never thought of that! And yes, I'm happy to not have other people's allergies entered into my home." This also makes you look like the professional (which you are) because you've thought of every aspect of how to protect your clients. Some people will say, "But I'm clean, I promise I won't damage your items." You'll have to stick to your guns because when you have a team, if you flip flop, are always changing your mind and making

---

[4] http://www.pestworld.org/news-and-views/pest-articles/articles/six-facts-you-didnt-know-about-bed-bugs/

exceptions, they will get confused and something nasty is bound to get staged.

YOUR OWN:
Occupied Staging Consultations

Occupied Consultation Style: _____

Duration of Consultation (time): _____

Will you offer written reports? If so, how?

Will you offer accessory rentals? On what condition?

Step 1 – Prior to Consultation:

Step 2 – During the Consultation:

Step 3 – After the Consultation:

Inventory Rental or Resale Protocol:

YOUR OWN:
Decorating Consultations

Decorating Consultation Style: _____

Duration of Consultation (time): _____

Will you offer written reports? If so, how?

Will you offer accessory rentals? On what condition?

Step 1 – Prior to Consultation:

Step 2 – During the Consultation:

Step 3 – After the Consultation:

Inventory Rental or Resale Protocol:

The next important sheet I use is our **"Staging Project Sheet"** This form is pre-printed and kept in the office with our consultation packages that includes a copy of our "Home Evaluation Consultation Book" Outlined on **page 81** and a copy of our home owner agreement / contract outlining that we were at the appointment. I try and pre-fill out all of the customers information BEFORE the appointment so I am prepared with the client name, contact information and special notes before entering the home.

CHSD Job Checklist

Client: _____   Date of Job: _____
Phone#: _____   Email: _____
Job Address: _____
Agent: _____   CC on File: YES NO – OBTAIN
Job Type: _____   Assigned Stager: _____
Pre Job
Notes: _____
_____
_____
_____

2hr in house consultation (✓)
    Payment Collected (Home Owners only) □   Agreement collected □ (Attach)
    Showcasing Required □   Inventory Required □
Job
Notes: _____
_____
_____
_____
_____

After Job Duties 1hr

Task	✓	Notes
Review email to Realtor with 12 hrs of job		CC info@chsd.ca & accounting@chsd.ca
Suggested Showcase Package: 1_____, 2_____, 3_____		Follow up in 2 days to book apt.
Send Before photos to office (Subject – address)		info@chsd.ca
Obtain AFTER photos from webpage send to office		info@chsd.ca
Request Testimonial from Home Owner & Agent		Send to accounting@chsd.ca & CC info@chsd.ca

If required for the job submit a quote within 24hrs.
Post Job Notes: _____
_____
_____
_____
_____

SEND THIS PAGE & THE HANDBOOK AGREEMENT SIGNED TOGETHER BACK TO HQ

Version 0.2 2014 KM

Vacant Consultations

Vacants are my favourite service we provide is for empty homes. These are not only the most profitable for us but so easy to do when we don't have to work around clients horrible decor items. First we start off with our client forms, we actually use the SAME client forms as we do for our occupied staging consultations because it has all the necessary information we require for the initial consultation. This also reduces the number of papers I had to create, track and update as my business grew.

The I had to establish what I wanted to get out of the consultation. I learned early on the MORE questions you ask the clients the more you control the appointment and are likely to win the job. If you let the client do all the talking then they generally feel like they can do the work on their own since you had nothing to say. I always do goal setting with the home owner; How long has your home been on the market for? Are you listing with a realtor or FSBO? Are you open to learning about the BEST way to position your home for a quick sale? What is your target list price for the home? Is that considered fair market value? What has been the current feedback for this home when buyers come to view it? Are you wanting to work with a company that has the cheapest rates or a company that knows what it takes to get a home sold fast and for top dollar? (I usually joke that cheap isn't good, and good isn't cheap) most respond with wanting a happy medium result.

Next we choose to take photos of the rooms we are staging from the corner of each room to ensure we can see every wall. Our team has been in so many homes that we know what will fit by just looking at a wall however if you are new you'll want to take your time and take measurements of the main walls, window / door way positions and the stairs so you are prepared for proper structure of bedding (full mattress or split)

Once we have evaluated the space and determined the rooms the client wants us to stage we go back to the office do a review of the photos to ensure we didn't miss anything during our walkthrough and provide our clients with a pricing sheet. Here we have created 4 "pre-made" staging packages based on the number of rooms staged. Some stagers prefer to do custom quotes every time but that is quite time consuming and in my market we found that every single apartment we quoted was about $2000. Their is only so much that can fit into a room I'll show you shortly how we created our pre-made staging packages that we can edit prior to sending to our clients to maximize our ROI (return on investment)

Capital Home Staging & Design

WHAT TO DO document

Task: VHSC – Vacant Home Staging Consultation

Positions involved: Property Stylist (PS)

Office will make appointment and provide Job Sheet.

- Arrive and discuss with the homeowner what their goals are for the property.
- Explain the importance of staging and share some CHSD stats with the homeowner.
- Evaluate the property's condition and write down suggestions.
- Evaluate space and determine what major pieces need to be in the home.
- Take photos of the property
- Take measurements of the space if required

After the appointment:
- Complete the "VACANT HOME STAGING PROPOSAL"
  - o Into to owner
  - o Suggestions for property

- o Statistics on vacant properties
- o Provide a quote
- Email proposal to the homeowner in PDF Format

Within 24 hrs:
- Follow-up with homeowner to discuss and officially book **(what are we booking?)** if proposal is accepted.
- Discuss with client the need for a 100% payment upfront to reserve inventory. We do this because from approval to set up is 7 days and chasing after people for payment is timely.
- Ensure client understands that there are no refunds or cancellation on the one month agreement. Owner may cancel after the 1st month is complete.

Once deposit is acquired:
- Confirm a date and time with homeowner for set-up at the property
- Update calendar with appointment and notify office that inventory will be going out on this job
- Officially select the inventory for the property

Prior to the set-up date:
- Wrap and pack inventory for delivery
- If we are using National pieces make arrangements for delivery

Deliver pieces and stage property

Following the Staging:
- Enter property into G-Docs Vacant Property tracking sheet
- Monitor property on a monthly basis and contact homeowner to determine renewal date and obtain fee or schedule pick-up.

Note:
- Initial property visit is 30-45 minutes

- Putting the proposal together with the written report is 1.5hrs

YOUR OWN:
Vacant Consultations

Vacant Consultation Style: _____

Duration of Consultation (time): _____

Will you offer written reports? If so, how?

Will you offer accessory rentals? On what condition?

Step 1 – Prior to Consultation:

Step 2 – During the Consultation:

Step 3 – After the Consultation:

Inventory Rental or Resale Protocol:

Next step is to generate a quote. We used to spend many hours to create custom quotes for every single home we consulted on, but it was taking us an easy 1-2hr each time and when you are quoting more and more homes, this is an easy time waster. I quickly became fed-up with spending my evenings creating custom quotes for everyone, which ended up being within $100.00 of the previous similar sized job, so we automated our quoting systems by creating pre-made staging packages. This was a result of noticing a trend in our pricing. We first priced out the most expensive living room for an apartment, then townhome, detached home with an open concept, and a large single home. This resulted in a clear pricing for living rooms, based on the size of the home.

For me to price out our jobs, I wrote a list of what I generally require in each room, starting with the most expensive, the living room.

Couch	$120	Area Rug	$45
2 Chairs OR Love seat	$100	3 Large Art / Mirror	$100
Coffee & Ends	$75	Large accessory kit	$200
2 Lamps	$50		

TOTAL Inventory for 1 living room space: $690

I did this process for every room I could possibly stage in a home and grouped them into 4 levels of packages. Once you have determined the room price for all the common rooms, with varying sizes for each category of home, you'll want to calculate your moving & staging costs. For us, I know that we can be in and out of a job in 10hrs, so I price my jobs at 15hrs to allot for unforeseen circumstances (which can happen often during the busy season).

In my packages, I include "free" elements that look like bonuses. These are small things that don't cost a lot to stage and because I have the pricing balance, I still have good profit margins in the end.

Package 1 (Photo on page 163)
- Stage 3 main rooms with furniture & decor
  - living, dining, master
- Stage 3 small rooms with just accessories
  - kitchen & bath / hallways

Package 2
- Stage 4 main rooms with furniture & decor
  - living, dining, master, kitchen
- Stage 3 small rooms with just accessories
  - bathrooms / hallways

Package 3
- Stage 5 main rooms with furniture & decor
  - living, dining, master, family room, kitchen
- Stage 4 small rooms with just accessories
  - bathrooms / hallways

Package 4
- Stage 6 main rooms with furniture & decor
  - living, dining, master, family, formal dining, kitchen
- Stage 5 small rooms with just accessories
  - bathrooms / hallways

Client needs a Package 4, but not the entire five accessory rooms? No problem! Keep your pricing, but delete the room numbers to suit your needs for that specific client. You just increased your profit margins right there by keeping your pricing the same and deleting the rooms not required BEFORE you sent it to the client for approval. Having these pre-made packages that have clear pricing and benefits will reduce your quoting and processing times and make for quick final adjustments as necessary just before sending it out to the client.

As soon as I created pre-made quotes, I freed up my evenings and weekends immediately and I also increased my profit margins by being effective in knowing what my base pricing is and how to price the rest accordingly so we don't lose money.

Capital Home
Staging & Design

Capital Home Staging & Design
613-832-8958 | info@chsd.ca
www.CapitalHomeStagingAndDesign.ca

Vacant Package

This package is suitable for small apartments and small condo's. The key to getting a property SOLD is to create an emotional response and connection in the decision making rooms. We believe in staging homes right the first time so they sell not only quicker but for top dollar.

Inclusions: 3 Decision Making Rooms

1) **Living Room**
   Couch, 2 chairs, area rug, coffee table set, lamps, decorative accessories package -small, art package.
2) **Dining Room**
   5pc dining set, art package, decorative accessories.
3) **Master Bedroom**
   Queen bed, headboard, boxspring, mattress, lamps, end tables, linen kit, pillow kit, decorative accessories package -small, art.
4) **Kitchen Accessories Kit -Small** (no furniture)
5) **Services Included**
   - 30 min initial home preview prior to sourcing items
   - Team of 3-4 staging professionals & moving men.
   - Delivery, carry in, assembly, future take down & removal.
   - Custom inventory selection to target market this property.
   - Coordination of delivery & future pick up.
   - Room configuration & design to maximize the wow factor.
   - Light cleaning of products brought in.

CHSD Exclusive Bonus:
   -FREE Professional photos for proper listings.
   -FREE Entrance staging to ensure an immediate welcome feeling.
   -FREE Bathroom stagings (up to 2 rooms)
   -FREE Hallway staging leading to staged rooms.
   -FREE Drapery rental if rods are supplied if required.

Professional Photos!

By iPro Tours.
additional tours, and videos may be added on directly through iPro Tours.

Terms & Rates

Inventory rental is cycled in 30 day terms. If renewal of inventory is required the fee is due four days in advance of the due date.

Initial Staging Investment: $1997.00
Monthly Inventory Renewal Rate: $1105.00

Approximate Inventory Value: $15,000.00*
*Based on the average retail value of all furniture & decor professionally sourced in a home this size.

Our award winning team is here to help you get your property transformed to SELL!

160

Know Your Pricing

Do you have a local furniture rental company? _____

Will you use their pricing structure? _____

If not, what percentage will you rent your furniture out at?
(suggestion: 25% of retail value at a minimum so it's paid off after 4 rentals)

Will you include professional photography?
_____YES (price: $_____, company:_____
_____NO

Pricing Matrix

Item	Rental Price	Item	Rental Price
Couch		Area Rug	
2 chair / love seat		3 Large Art / Mir	
Coffee & Ends		Accessory Kit <50 items	

2 Lamps	
Dining table & chairs (6-8pc)	2 Large Art / Mir
Hutch	Accessory Kit <20 items
Queen Bed Set	Bedding / pillows
2 Night Tables	3 Large Art / Mir
2 Lamps	Accessory Kit <50 items
Dresser	
Kitchen accessories <75 items.	Bathroom Kits (Towels, Art, Accessories)
DELIVERY FEE	STAGING FEE

The pricing matrix will allow you to easily view your CORE costs; if you have a home that requires 2 living spaces, then take the total cost of the living area you priced out and multiply by 2. Each living space will generally fit a specific amount of furniture. The beauty is if we need MORE, we can adjust our pre-made quotes before they are sent out. You will also want to take into consideration if your supplier requires you to rent for a minimum number of months. Here in Ottawa, our supplier is on an exclusive month-to-month agreement in our pricing structure.

We have packages for apartments, townhomes, bungalows, and detached homes. As for all LUXURY homes, we choose to price per home because the quality and amount of furniture required is extremely subjective per property. The most I ever quoted and won on a luxury custom quote was $20,000 + tax, paid upfront. The realtor was super on-board with the entire process and really helped with discussing the importance of staging this luxury home that was considered "unsellable" for four years with another realtor. After we staged the home, it sold in 2 days for $15,000 over asking price, how amazing is that!? We were happy we won the large job, the realtor was happy it sold fast, and the homeowner was happy that, not only it sold fast, but they sold it $15K over asking price.

Take an afternoon to create the 4 packages that you'll use as a primary template.

Package 1
Total furniture rental price: _____
Delivery Fee (drop off & pick up): _____
Staging Fee (inventory pulling, staging & pick up): _____
Target MAX hours on this job: _____

Package 2
Total furniture rental price: _____
Delivery Fee (drop off & pick up): _____
Staging Fee (inventory pulling, staging & pick up): _____
Target MAX hours on this job: _____

Package 3
Total furniture rental price: _____
Delivery Fee (drop off & pick up): _____
Staging Fee (inventory pulling, staging & pick up): _____
Target MAX hours on this job: _____

Package 4
Total furniture rental price: _____
Delivery Fee (drop off & pick up): _____

Staging Fee (inventory pulling, staging & pick up): _____
Target MAX hours on this job: _____

<u>**Package 5**</u>
Total furniture rental price: _____
Delivery Fee (drop off & pick up): _____
Staging Fee (inventory pulling, staging & pick up): _____
Target MAX hours on this job: _____

Now that we have most of our pricing under wraps, we'll move onto one of the most popular topics when I do my chat: how do you pull inventory to be fast and efficient? With SYSTEMS of course! When you have a clear system, it's easy to pull fast and quick. We have a system where we list every table top / surface we need to pull an accessory for, from end tables to fireplace mantles. We have a simple version here and as you are pulling inventory, you'll write in the space what you pulled so you know you have enough items for all the surfaces in the home. It's just a matter of placing them or switching them out when you're in the home for the right look.

<u>*Living Room*</u>
End Table 1: (lamp) +_____
End Table 2: (lamp) +_____
Coffee Table Top: _____
Bottom Shelf: _____
Fireplace Mantle: _____
Hearth: _____
Art Above Couch: _____
Above Mantle: _____
Other Areas: _____

<u>*Formal Living Room*</u>
End Table 1: (lamp) +_____
End Table 2: (lamp) +_____
Coffee Table Top: _____
Bottom Shelf: _____
Fireplace Mantle: _____

Hearth: _____

Art Above Couch: _____

Above Mantle: _____

Other Areas: _____

Dining Room
Table Centrepiece: _____

Tops of Hutches: _____

Art Above Hutch: _____

Main Art Focal: _____

Other / Tall Decor: _____

Formal Dining Room
Table Centrepiece: _____

Tops of Hutches: _____

Art Above Hutch: _____

Main Art Focal: _____

Other / Tall Decor: _____

Master Bedroom
Night Table 1: (lamp) +_____

Night Table 2: (lamp) + _____

Dresser Top: _____

Art Near Bed 1-2: _____

Above Dresser: _____

Side Table: (if req.) _____

Kitchen
Counter 1 Decor: _____

Counter 2 Decor: _____

Island Decor: _____

Art 1-2: _____

Centrepiece for Bistro / Eat-in Area: _____

Bathroom Kit #1
3pc Towel Set X _____ in colour _____

Vanity Accessories: _____

Art Piece: _____

Bathroom Kit #2
3pc Towel Set X _____ in colour _____
Vanity Accessories: _____
Art Piece: _____

Kids Bedroom #1
Night Table 1: (lamp) +_____
Night Table 2: (lamp) + _____
Dresser Top: _____
Art Near Bed 1-2: _____
Above Dresser: _____
Side Table: (if req.) _____

To make pulling jobs easier, I created a 1 page document listing 2 living rooms, 2 dining rooms, the master bedroom, 1 kids room, kitchen and 2 bathrooms, printed out 25 copies, and I leave them in my warehouse for easy reference and pulling when ready. This will dramatically cut your pulling time in half and stop you from second guessing your choices. Once you have the entire sheet filled out, you'll know 100% that you have enough decor pulled to fill EACH surface in the home properly. I also have a "Bonus Bin", a bin of accessories that I can reference to or go through at the END of the staging job if I feel something is missing or I need a different focal point.

Next is our job sheet that I'm going to review for vacant set-ups. This is a two-sided sheet where the 1st side helps me coordinate the workings of the staging job: who the lead stager is, who the assistants are, if the movers are booked and for when, if the photographer is booked and for when, as well as any specific job notes. I also have a generic checklist as to what EACH person's duties are per job.

The 2nd page is the most important page. I call it our fail-safe checklist, ensuring that nothing is left unturned upon our final staging walkthrough. If temperature was adjusted or windows were opened, this checklist will make you walk through each room and check off that you change back everything to the way it was before. I also have a list of common issues I find in each room when I'm not there, due to a "rushed job", and we don't want our jobs to ever appear as rushed. This can be inside out bed skirts / sheets, lampshade seams visible, crooked artwork, uncleaned windows, mirrors or glass tables, etc. Be creative here, what drives you NUTS when you walk into a room? Put it on the list, this way your entire team will know not to make the mistake.

Vacant StagingSet Up Checklist

Capital Home
Staging & Design

STAGERS should work individually in each room to complete the staging as fast as possible. The assistant stager should be creative enough to complete a room without the help of the lead stager. It is the duty of the lead stager to review the room and change any things they do not like. Upon the final review by KRISTY a final edit may happen if required. Once the initial staging is completed then the lead stager and assistant can go through together evaluating and making changes if necessary

Booking Overview

Date of Staging: _____
Address: _____

Lead Stager: _____
Assistant: _____
Runner(optional): _____

- [ ] Contracts signed & received.
- [ ] Payment form signed & received.
- [ ] Payment collected 3-7 days before job. Note: cheques must be cleared before booking (7 days to clear)

Movers Booked: _____
    Date/Time: _____

Photographers Booked: _____
    Date/Time: _____

Staging Package: _____
    Copy printed & attached?   Y / N

PICK UP Scheduled: _____

Notes: _____
_____
_____
_____
_____
_____
_____
_____
_____
_____
_____
_____
_____
_____

Lead Stager Duties

- [ ] Advise movers of where furniture is to be placed.
- [ ] Advise assistant what you want them to do in the home. (what room should they set up)
- [ ] Pick a room and start staging -generally the hardest room in the house.

Assistant Stager Duties

- [ ] Unpack the accessories in 1 room generally the kitchen while the lead stager advises movers where furniture is to be placed.
- [ ] Foresee Lead stager needs & help.
- [ ] Assist with drapery hanging
- [ ] Ironing / steaming
    - [ ] Bedding & Pillows
    - [ ] Shower curtains
    - [ ] Any soft item that is wrinkled
- [ ] Take photos of the rooms staged and texted or emailed to KRISTY for review BEFORE LEAVING incase changes need to be made.
- [ ] Dust & windex all surfaces
    - [ ] Tables -All.
    - [ ] Mirrors we added & bathrooms
    - [ ] Anything with marks.

Runner's Duties

- [ ] To assist the lead stager and assistant stager.
- [ ] Run and grab items the team needs.
- [ ] Removal of excess bins and decor from home.
- [ ] Assist the Assistant with ALL duties above when requested

Final Walk-Through Checklist- Before Professional Photo's

Capital Home
Staging & Design

OVERALL

- [ ] All Table tops are dusted & shined
- [ ] All Lights On -Accent Lighting
- [ ] Blinds are even & proper hight -no negative views outside.
- [ ] Lamp Shades are Even & seams hidden.
- [ ] Extension cords are out of sight.
- [ ] Lights requiring an extension cord has one.
- [ ] ALL mirrors are streak-free.
- [ ] Entrance is swept from tracked in debris.
- [ ] All Staging Items are removed from home.
- [ ] *Staging Marketing Triangle & 10 business cards left in the kitchen (lead stager only)*

Living Room

- [ ] Sofa is in proper position in relation to the focal point in the room.
- [ ] Sofa connected to rug, coffee table is centred on sofa.
- [ ] Microfibre is all in 1 direction (all furniture)
- [ ] Tags Not Showing on pillows or throws.
- [ ] Pillows on sofa are straight & positioned properly.
- [ ] Chairs are appropriately angled / positioned in relation to the rooms flow & focal point.
- [ ] Rug's are not rolled or wrinkled.
- [ ] Light vacuuming if required is done.
- [ ] Art is even & clean / streak-free.

Bed Rooms

- [ ] Bed Skirt liner is not showing
- [ ] Bed Skirt & fitted sheet is not inside out.
- [ ] Bedding, Skirt, Pillows are wrinkle free.
- [ ] Pictures are even & properly positioned.
- [ ] Lamps have bulbs & are on.
- [ ] Closet Door Closed if not staged.

Bathrooms

- [ ] Toilet Seats Down
- [ ] Towels are folded -edges to the centre and positioned centred on the rack.
- [ ] Shower curtain is wrinkle free.
- [ ] Pictures are even & properly positioned.

BEFORE YOU LEAVE

- [ ] All Staging bins & tools are removed from the home.
- [ ] All Lights Off.
- [ ] Temperature is re-adjusted to original settings if changed during the staging.
- [ ] Alarm is set (if their is one)
- [ ] All Windows are closed -GO LOOK
- [ ] All Back & Side doors are closed -GO LOOK
- [ ] Front door is LOCKED
- [ ] Key is returned to the lockbox.
- [ ] Photograph any home issues for record keeping. Advise Operations to determine if it's an issue to present.
- [ ] Advise agent the staging is done.

Notes:
_____
_____
_____
_____
_____
_____
_____
_____
_____
_____
_____
_____
_____
_____
_____
_____
_____

Photographer's #: Andrew 613-862-2208
andrewo@iprotours.com

Property of Capital Home Staging & Design -Copy-write 2015

To Warehouse or Not to Warehouse

This is going to be the hardest thing for me to help you with because the cost of warehouses will vary all over North America. I have friends who have warehouse space in the States and they have 5,000 sq ft for about $2,000 a month. I have a 2,000 sq ft warehouse and I'm currently paying $2,700, so I'm paying MORE for significantly LESS space, just because I live in one of the most expensive cities for business owners to operate in. So for me to properly help you answer this question, we'll need to define some of your current principles.

- Do you currently own your own furniture or decor?
    - _____YES _____NO
- Is your furniture continually out making you income?
    - _____YES _____NO
- Is your spouse getting angry with stuff all over?
    - _____YES _____NO
- RESEARCH
    - Self-storage pricing per sq ft: _____
    - Warehouse pricing per sq ft: _____

- Based on 2,000 sq ft, can you afford the monthly rental fee?
    - _____YES _____NO
- How about hidden fees? Heat? Hydro? Security?
    - _____YES _____NO
- Can you manage a warehouse, inventory, storage?
    - _____YES _____NO

Based on the above questions and your business outline we worked through at the beginning of the book, only YOU can decide if you should make the jump to having a true warehouse space. For myself, I used my garage for the first 1.5 years, then I moved to a self-storage unit where I had 500 sq ft for $800 a month, and when I needed a 2nd storage unit for a total of 1000 sq ft for $1600 a month, I decided to make the jump and purchase a warehouse space of 2000 sq ft. I took over only the main floor of 1000 sq ft and had a tenant rent the second floor of 1000 sq ft. for 70% of the total costs. I kept my square footage, but ended up paying $600 LESS by moving and obtaining a tenant.

BONUS NOTE: I don't suggest purchasing a commercial space because, in Canada, we need to have a minimum 20% down payment for all properties outside your primary residence. This is a MASSIVE amount of capital gone, and as a fast-growing business that wants to obtain more and more jobs as well as inventory, then you will outgrow the space QUICKLY. Also, when it comes to moving and selling a property (we are currently going through this now), it is a much different ball game than with a residential property. Finding a buyer, negotiating the terms and having a quick move out of 15-20 days, plus having to find another location and quickly set up into it, is extremely hard to coordinate, especially when business is operational.

Ultimately, I suggest growing your business slowly. Over time, as you're growing, start with home storage, move to self-storage and eventually have a true warehouse storage.

TODD'S TIDBIT FOR THURSDAY...
By Todd McAllister of On Stage Home Staging.
This was originally posted on his Home Stagers Facebook group.

There have been a lot of people getting larger warehouse spaces recently. AND THAT IS VERY EXCITING! Here are a few things to consider when looking for a space...

1. Look for a space that is off the beaten path. For the most part, stagers are not a destination business. Finding a space in an unusual location can save lots of money.
2. Having a loading dock of some type will speed up the process of loading / unloading a truck.
3. Look for a space you can GROW INTO. Think about the future growth of your business. (But don't do too big to start.)

4. Normally, office space is calculated at a higher rate than warehouse space. Make sure you actually need that 1,000 sq ft office space. You will pay a lot to have it.
5. What utilities are you responsible for?
6. Ask for free rent. The standard is: for every year you lease, you should get one month of free rent. BUT THIS IS NOT ALWAYS THE CASE.
7. Is the location convenient for the area you service?
8. Like a house inspection, I would suggest having an inspection by a third party for all mechanical systems. If there is a problem, who will fix it?
9. DO NOT BE AFRAID TO NEGOTIATE THE PRICE PER SQ FT.

I hope a few of these suggestions will help in your next warehouse search. Have a GREAT DAY from Portland.

Kristy Morrison

Inventory Storage Systems

Great storage is the key to protecting one of your assets in your business. If you are not handy, it's worth it to hire someone to help build a custom rack storage system for all your furniture. Our warehouse has 3-tier wood shelving racks: the main floor is the ground where all heavy items are kept like dressers, buffet hutches, couches, etc. The 2nd tier is covered in leftover carpet from a flooring store; they generally have miscellaneous coloured garbage carpet that is new and can be used for protection. We store coffee & end tables, night tables and chairs all stacked and nestled together to maximize space. The top tier is about 10 feet off the floor, so we tend to keep items not frequently used up here, like items specific for trade shows, excess storage bins / boxes, etc.

Artwork is stored in the same manner, with custom racks. Top shelves, covered in carpet chunks, will house the small artwork 10x10 in size, the next shelf below is for medium art pieces and the bottom shelf is for the large art and mirror pieces. To protect the artwork and the frames, we use the foam boards we get from unpacking furniture and put them in-between each art piece on top of covering each one in plastic. We've also used cardboard slats to prevent the back hooks from scratching nestled pieces.

Our accessories are stored on metal shelving purchased at Home Depot. Shelves are made of wood and solid so items don't fall through the cracks, the height is also adjustable to accommodate different sizing of decor items. We organize items based on ROOM & COLOUR. All kitchen items are grouped on a shelf (or two), then subgrouped by colour, same goes for bathroom items. All accessories that can be used in either a living, dining, or bedroom are just grouped by colour for easy pulling.

Literally, setting up a warehouse for maximum efficiency should be a course on its own. You can find out great information by following stagers on the RESA and STAGERS LIKE US Facebook pages.

Essential Tools for Inventory Protection

✓ Moving Blankets (buy in bulk from local moving stores, about $6-12 each.)
✓ Plastic Wrap (to wrap all furniture)
✓ Sharpie markers (black & metallic)
✓ Coloured duct tape
✓ Masking tape
✓ Rolling feet

uline.com is a BRILLIANT packaging store that sells everything you could possibly need to protect and organize your warehouse.

MY FAVOURITE TIPS

* Lamps are stored on metal racks, the base on the main shelf with the shade on the top shelf.
* Transportation of lamps: we use the Home Sense / Home Goods reusable bags with a hard plastic foam on the BOTTOM of the bag. Lamps are placed on top of the foam side by side. For protection when moving, we pack in our throw blankets in-between the lamps so they don't bang around. ALL lamps are transported in our cars (never the movers' truck) and seat belted into position like a baby. Shades are off the lamps in plastic bags to prevent damage.
* Couches are standing on their side to maximize on floor space.
* Bins are packed for each room & labeled accordingly. So once the living room is pulled, it all goes in a plastic bin wrapped in foam / paper and labelled "Main Living Room". This allows the movers to carry all items into each specific room.
* Moving blankets are frequently "stolen" by accident by movers since they all look similar. Use a fabric spray paint to identify your blankets clearly. CHOOSE HOT PINK because

no moving man wants pink in their truck (or so I've been told).

* Pillows are stored on metal racks in rows of colours.
* Bathroom & kitchen accessories each have their own shelf to ensure grouping is easy for pulling.
* Rugs are stored on a custom shelf, rolled up and grouped by size and colour. Heavy rugs on the bottom, smaller rugs higher on top.
* Artwork is stored in racks with carpet protection and foam boards between each art piece.
* General accessories are stored all in the same area, but in coloured groups.

We have created a quick reference sheet as to what is acceptable storage in our warehouse. This is printed and left on the wall at the unit for all to see.

Proper Storage

WRONG   RIGHT

When product is stored unwrapped it scratches with natural dirt.

Capital Home
Staging & Design

175

ALL Items must be covered with a blanked and stored table top to table top to avoid scratches on the surface of the items

WRONG

RIGHT

Couches are to be stored with the appropriate cushions intact and wrapped on 1 side with a blanked and entirely wrapped in plastic. All of our couches are stored vertically on their ends to save on space and the blankets protect the fabric of the couch. Chairs covered and stored nestled on respective couches.
How do you want your warehouse storage to look like?

WRONG

RIGHT

Couches:_____

Chairs & Small Tables:_____

Dining Tables (Glass):_____

Dining Tables (Wood):_____

Rugs:_____

Artwork:_____

Mirrors:_____

Pillows:_____

Bed Pillows:_____

Curtains:_____

Plants (Short):_____

Plants (Tall):_____

Bedding Sets:_____

Bathroom Acc:_____

Kitchen Acc:_____

General Acc:_____

_____

_____

_____

_____

Other:_____

_____

_____

_____

_____

_____

Darby Inventory System

I've searched long and hard for an inventory program that's specific to a stager's needs. Most inventory systems are for SALES, meaning you can purchase 5 couches and when they go out, then it's considered a sale and they are gone, they never come back into stock as a "restocked" item. This is not ideal for our type of business, we need to know how often a product goes in and out for a job. If it's a hot commodity, then we can order more; if it's a dud, we can sell it off and never order the item again.

I started using Darby 1 year into having my business. Tammie and her team were amazing and helped enter all the products. I just wish I had started with them from day one; entering things as I grow my inventory is always easier in an evolution progress than a dumping progress.

Register at: **www.MyDarby.com** (referral code CHSD)

First, you'll want to set up the **ROOMS** so when you enter inventory, they can be categorized by rooms and easily found upon pick up. These are the room titles we use:

Family Room	Dining Room	Formal Living	Formal Dining
Master Bedroom	Kids Room 1	Kids Room 2	Kids Room 3
Ensuite Bath	Main Bath	Powder Room 1	Powder Room 2
Basement Main	Theater Room	Laundry Room	In-Law Suite
In-Law Bath	Loft	Office	Other

Next, we will want to set up inventory categories for each of the items the inventory will be placed into. Again, we use the following categories:

Living Room	Dining Room	Bedroom	Other
-Couches	-Tables	-Queen Bed	-Desk &
-Love Seat	-Chairs	-King Bed	Office Chairs
-Chairs	-Hutches	-Children's	-Occasional
-Coffee &		Bed	Tables
Ends		-Bed Rails	-Accent
-Sofa Tables		-Mattress &	Furniture
		Box	

Accessories	Artwork	Soft	Rugs
-Vases tall	-Small	**Accessories**	-5x7
-Vases small	-Medium	-Pillows Full	-8x10
-Candles	-Large	-Pillows Half	-Odd Sizes
-Candle	-Mirrors	-Pillows Bed	
Stands		-Curtains 84"	
-Kitchen		-Curtains 93"	
Decor		-Bedding	
-Bathroom		Queen	
Decor		-Bedding King	
-Bowls		-Runners &	
-Bowl Fillers		Cloths	

Once we have those sections set up in our inventory program, we'll need to set up inventory key codes. This will be the basis of each category code. Darby has a default that at the end of the code, if you enter * then it will automatically generate the next available number in the system, i.e.: COUCH* = COUCH24.

I suggest printing a copy of the inventory codes chart and leaving it by your computer and at the warehouse so should you require a quick entry, you won't have to dig for this handy sheet. Darby also offered barcode scanning capabilities so 90% of our inventory is coded and the other 10% is in progress due to quick purchasing and having to get it out on a job fast. In order to ensure we provide the right code for each item, we always write the inventory code on the item so later on I can print the sticker. I also write "Property of CHSD" meaning Property of Capital Home Staging & Design. This way no one can claim that it is possibly their decor item. Here's an example of the codes we use:

-COUCH*	-DINE T*	-Q BED*	-DESK*
-CHAIR*	-DINE	-K BED*	-OFFCH*
-COFFEE T*	CHAIR*	-CH BED*	-OCC T*
-END T*	-HUTCH*	-BED RAILS*	-ACCFURN*
-CE T SET*		-MATBOX*	
-SOFA T*			
-ACC-VASE*	-ART-SM*	-PILLOW-F*	RUG5*
-ACC-CDL*	-ART-MD*	-PILLOW-H*	RUG8*
-CDSTICK*	-ART-LG*	-PILLOW-	RUG-ODD*
-ACC-KIT*	-MIRROR*	BD*	
-ACC-BATH*		-CURT84*	
-ACC-		-CURT93*	
BOWL*		-LIN-Q*	
-ACC-FILL*		-LIN-K*	
		-RUNNER*	

On the next page, I've provided 2 of the 17-page inventory document for ONE staging job we have performed. As you can see, this allows for easy pick up of the job because we see the location the item was left in (based on the photos taken once we finished staging). Now, how MANY of the items were left on the job? For example, our towels are grouped in 3pc sets; bath and hand towels and a face cloth are one set, so if in a bathroom it says 2 sets, then that means in that room we should have a total of 6 towels there.

When you print these pull sheets, you have the option of printing

Capital Home Staging & Design
2729 Kelly Ave
Ottawa, on K2B7V2
p: (613) 832-8958
www.CapitalHomeStagingAndDesign.ca

Diane Wallace
Order Date: 01/23/2016
Type: Rental/Lease

Sales Order
SO#: 00000166

Bill To: Minto Communities
90 Sheppard Ave. East
Toronto

Ship To: 1035 Bank Stree
unit 101
Ottawa

		Product	Qty	Product #	Sale Price	Total Price
	Bathroom - Ensuite					
1		stylized row bo... stylized row boat -modern art, canvas with dark frame	1		$120.00	$120.00
2		Angled wood 3 s... book shelf	1		$150.00	$150.00
3		Silver Coral St... Silver Coral Statue, flat free standing made of metal	1		$60.00	$60.00
4		Medium Silver S... Medium Silver Sail Boat one is smooth one is rough	1		$30.00	$30.00
5		2pc Silver Boat... 2pc Silver Sail Boats	2		$25.00	$50.00
6		Silver Box rect... 	1		$30.00	$30.00
7		Set of 3 Apothe... 	1		$80.00	$80.00

		Product	Qty	Product #	Sale Price	Total Price
	Living Room Formal					
1		Silver Crackle ... Silver Crackle Lamp with Black Shade	2		$80.00	$160.00
2		Silver metal dr... Silver metal drum end table looks like dents	2		$59.99	$119.98
3		Yellow open flo... Clear square vase	1		$14.99	$14.99
4		ball, vase + st... 3pc Blue candle set	2		$17.00	$34.00
5		1/2 grey & Whit... 1/2 grey & White pattern pillow, modern, sexy	2		$45.00	$90.00
6		Grey & White Ot... Grey & White Ottoman, zig zag, Eric Set	1		$200.00	$200.00
7		Rectangle Mirro...	1		$130.00	$130.00
8		Brown & Silver ... Brown & Silver Vase	1		$25.00	$25.00
9		White ceramic a... White ceramic Artichoke	1		$15.00	$15.00

SCREEN SHOT of 4 jobs worth of inventory entered and identified with a checkmark as currency out.

SCREEN SHOT of our couches inventory you can see how many on hand, contracted on a job and committed means it's been identified as needed for a job but the job hasn't gone out yet. I also like the photo capabilities of inventory to easily identify which couch is which.

Social Media

Automated Social Media

EVERY BUSINESS NEEDS TO HAVE AN ONLINE PRESENCE IN TODAY'S WORLD AND STANDARDS OF BUSINESS! I can't stress this enough. Potential clients will always Google the company they are interested in working with.

FACTS[5]

- ✓ 91% of local searches say they use Facebook to find a local business.
- ✓ 71% of social media participants say they are more likely to buy from a brand they follow online.
- ✓ Dedicating 5hrs a week on social media results in increased referrals.
- ✓ 350 million users suffer from Facebook addiction.
- ✓ Average user of Facebook has 130 friends.

If you use your Google calendar properly and SCHEDULE time to create and work on your social media presence, then it will make your life so much easier.

First things first, you'll need content. Where do you get content? There are many sources, such as:
- Your brilliant & creative mind
- Your home & friends' homes
- Industry partners: stores, paint, furniture, decor, etc.
- Colleagues all over the world (be sure to reference their work & give them recognition)

Start by following people in your industry and building relationships with them. For the most part, stagers don't mind if you "SHARE" their social content, as long as they are the ones that get the credit for the content. If you don't credit them, then it's technically IP theft.

---

[5] http://www.adweek.com/socialtimes/social-media-facts/482462

I like to work my social media accounts 3-6 months in advance, meaning I create content way before it's ever posted. This allows me to be efficient and not worry about what I'm going to post all the time. I treat it like a true social media SYSTEM.

The biggest thing I've heard from my fellow stagers is, "How do I give tips and create a social media campaign that doesn't give away the farm so to speak?" You'll all have to realize that we are sending out content of tips, facts and ideas in short bursts of knowledge all mixed together. It's literally impossible for someone to follow 100% of your posts and create direct competition for you or feel that you are not needed. As a matter of fact, when you provide so much content and tips, you'll increase business because there are so many factors to consider that it's overwhelming for the regular person. Honestly, if someone is willing to follow you with a microscope for years, to eventually try and do the work on their own, do you really want them as a client? They will probably try and micromanage your staging job, referencing OLD posts that you made over time. Don't worry about how much content you're sharing with the public, no one will be able to receive all the information and arrange it in an order that makes sense to them again.

The more networks you are on = the more interactions you will have = the more "klout" (online social influence) you will obtain = the more customers you will be attracting. Essentially, social media is a numbers' game to success.

Content creation

Start with the basic home staging **FACTS**. List them all from what home staging is NOT, to what home staging IS. Industry facts from realtors like, "Average unstaged home sells in over 120 days." (Know your local numbers, they are more powerful.) Look up facts on the RESA webpage and turn them into beautiful content. You should be able to create a list of 50 facts for your market easily.

Next, you'll want to create a list of **TIPS**, from how to hang curtains and art, how to create a photo wall, the best colours to use, your favourite places to shop, your favourite type of paint, creating a colour scheme and posting a photo, what is your favourite thing to use, etc. Literally, your tips can be absolutely anything, which is why they are the easiest to create. If you're having trouble, ask your friends and family for their most favourite home tips.

Here comes the easy part, **PHOTOS**! Every single one of you should be posting before and after photos. NOT just the afters because that is not where the power lies, it's in what the space looked like before you were involved and then what you made of it after. Here is a really cool tip for those of you who are just starting out and may only have a few photos: every room is a new transformation so you don't have to post them all as one house, you can post "Look at this beautifully transformed bedroom" or "Another stellar dining room". For the average staging job, you'll be able to get 5 before and after shots at a minimum (living room, dining room, master bedroom, kitchen & bath). So let's say, if you do 3 jobs a month each with 5 photos x 12 months of the year, that's 180 photos you can post!

Another easy one are the **HOLIDAY** posts. Every year I make specific posts for national holidays throughout the year. We have about 11 holidays & events we'll make posts for. Sometimes I'll even make multiple posts for a theme like Christmas.

Just with those 4 categories, you can have an easy posting list of 341 posts in 1 year. How amazing is that?! Our brains work much better when we batch tasks together, it allows us to focus, and so taking the time to pre-write and think about the content makes life much easier.

Many of you are probably questioning the 341 posts in a year time frame and are afraid that you'll be bugging people to no end shoving information down their throats, right? Wrong! Our reality has become fast-paced with short attention spans. Just because we are posting this much content, doesn't mean your prospects will see all of the information. Let's say someone on Facebook has only 5 friends, well in this case, they will see ALL of your posts because they don't have anyone else competing for space on your newsfeed. They will probably get annoyed, but don't fret, there is a clear "unfollow" button at the top of each Facebook page/profile, so people can use that if they feel they are obtaining too much content from you. Do not worry and keep on posting your beautiful and knowledgeable content. Your business will thank you for it!

ow, let's make your posts attractive! I use a very simple webpage called **canva.com** to create beautiful posts for Facebook, Instagram and Twitter. They are essentially just your data turned into a photo. On the next page, I've included a few examples of what I've created in the past. You can also view them in colour on my Facebook page **www.facebook.com/capitalhomestaginganddesign**.

Did you know that posts that contain photos, videos or links are the ones that get the most views and traction of shares than a generic written post? That's why I try and jazz up all of my social media posts with the Canva App. You can also use it to create beautiful banners and profile pics for all social media accounts.

Keep your posts and facts short and to the point, do not be too wordy or you will lose your audience in the message. You'll see what I mean with the next page of social media photos.

Now remember, I build my entire year of social media during my slow season. In December, at a very minimum, I spend time creating about 6 months' worth of content. The more I create, the less worry I have during the year of when/how to post. If I can't get an entire year of data written in my 1st slow month, then I'll write the rest during the summer, like at the end of August when it slows down again due to final summer holidays.

HOT TIP: When creating these photos, always be sure to include your webpage for your branding and as a way potential prospects can reach you. As I create beautiful photos of facts and tips, I save them in Dropbox in the order I want them launched: Tip1, Tip2, Tip3, Tip4, etc. This way I know I have enough content and I can see how it will fit in my program chart.

Now that you have beautiful photos to get your point across we'll need to get them launched to the public in a strategic manner. Automation is great for that, but it will only work when you have content produced and content needs time for it to be produced. So if you feel like you have no time, you definitely need an assistant to help with administrative tasks. And when I'm feeling really stuck, I recycle old posts, but add a fresh spin to it.

When automation comes into play, I use **hootsuite.com** to automate my Facebook and Twitter accounts. This is a very easy to use program that allows you to auto-populate your photos or links into a system that will launch your data at a specific date and time of your request.

In one year, we have 365 days which works out to be 52 weeks in a year. How are we going to fill those days and which days? Well, let's use the beauty of a hashtag (#). I love to use #TBT (Throw Back Thursdays) to reference old decor and start a conversation or #TipTuesday, there are so many you can create. The point of a hashtag is for you to be able to easily track the amount of shares your post are getting. Be patient, this won't happen overnight.

To begin mapping out my posting madness, I started with holiday topics. The frequency of this can be changed to fit the SPECIFIC day the holiday falls onto. If Christmas falls on a Wednesday, move the category to Wednesday, I am just using Monday as a place holder in the example on the next page.

For my **50 facts**, I'll add 2 more to equal a full year in weeks, and post on Fridays calling it #FactFriday. The **100 tips**, I add 4 more to complete the year of twice a week, and divide them into two posting times to make life easier; first is #TipTuesday that is delivered EVERY week, the next batch I sprinkle 26 on Thursdays and 26 on Saturdays under #CHSDTip. Finally, I will post my photos on Wednesdays under #Transform. As you grow your business, this part with photos will grow also, but you don't have to worry because in the meantime, you've already got GREAT content for Tuesday, Thursday, Friday & Saturday.

The following chart is my Facebook schedule, but what to do for Twitter?? Twitter is a fickle beast and will only allow 140 characters, so if any of your posts are wordy, it won't work. With any of my photos, I also automate using Twitter, but I will change the date so it looks like new content. Essentially when I plan my social media, for Facebook I post in order of 1-300 and for Twitter I'll post 300-1, working backwards so content is flipped and will look like new to the followers because, like I mentioned before, people will not see 100% of your posts. Also, many people who prefer Facebook do not use Twitter. As our primary social media outlet, we tend to gravitate to our preferred methods of media.

Social Media Posting Schedule

week	Monday	Tuesday	Wednesday	Thursday	Friday	Saturday
1	NewYears	#TipTues	#Transform	#CHSD Tip	#FactFri	
2		#TipTues	#Transform		#FactFri	#CHSD Tip
3		#TipTues	#Transform		#FactFri	
4		#TipTues	#Transform		#FactFri	
5		#TipTues	#Transform	#CHSD Tip	#FactFri	
6		#TipTues	#Transform		#FactFri	#CHSD Tip

7	Family D.	#TipTues	#Transform		#FactFri	
8		#TipTues	#Transform		#FactFri	
9		#TipTues	#Transform	#CHSD Tip	#FactFri	
10		#TipTues	#Transform		#FactFri	#CHSD Tip
11		#TipTues	#Transform		#FactFri	
12		#TipTues	#Transform		#FactFri	
13	Easter	#TipTues	#Transform	#CHSD Tip	#FactFri	
14	Mothers D.	#TipTues	#Transform		#FactFri	#CHSD Tip
15		#TipTues	#Transform		#FactFri	
16		#TipTues	#Transform		#FactFri	
17	Fathers D.	#TipTues	#Transform	#CHSD Tip	#FactFri	
18		#TipTues	#Transform		#FactFri	#CHSD Tip
19		#TipTues	#Transform		#FactFri	
20		#TipTues	#Transform		#FactFri	

		#TipTu es	#Transfo rm	#CHSD Tip	#FactFr i	
21		#TipTu es	#Transfo rm	#CHSD Tip	#FactFr i	
22		#TipTu es	#Transfo rm		#FactFr i	#CHSD Tip
23		#TipTu es	#Transfo rm		#FactFr i	
24		#TipTu es	#Transfo rm		#FactFr i	
25		#TipTu es	#Transfo rm	#CHSD Tip	#FactFr i	
26	Canada D.	#TipTu es	#Transfo rm		#FactFr i	#CHSD Tip
27		#TipTu es	#Transfo rm		#FactFr i	
28		#TipTu es	#Transfo rm		#FactFr i	
29		#TipTu es	#Transfo rm	#CHSD Tip	#FactFr i	
30		#TipTu es	#Transfo rm		#FactFr i	#CHSD Tip
31	Civic H.	#TipTu es	#Transfo rm		#FactFr i	
32		#TipTu es	#Transfo rm		#FactFr i	
33		#TipTu es	#Transfo rm	#CHSD Tip	#FactFr i	
34		#TipTu es	#Transfo rm		#FactFr i	#CHSD Tip

35		#TipTues	#Transform		#FactFri	
36	Labour D.	#TipTues	#Transform		#FactFri	
37		#TipTues	#Transform	#CHSDTip	#FactFri	
38		#TipTues	#Transform		#FactFri	#CHSDTip
39		#TipTues	#Transform		#FactFri	
40		#TipTues	#Transform		#FactFri	
41	Thanks G.	#TipTues	#Transform	#CHSDTip	#FactFri	
42		#TipTues	#Transform		#FactFri	#CHSDTip
43		#TipTues	#Transform		#FactFri	
44	Halloween	#TipTues	#Transform		#FactFri	
45		#TipTues	#Transform	#CHSDTip	#FactFri	
46		#TipTues	#Transform		#FactFri	#CHSDTip
47		#TipTues	#Transform		#FactFri	
48		#TipTues	#Transform		#FactFri	

49	**Christmas**	#TipTues	#Transform	#CHSDTip	#FactFri	
50	**Christmas**	#TipTues	#Transform		#FactFri	#CHSDTip
51	**Christmas**	#TipTues	#Transform		#FactFri	
52	Boxing Day	#TipTues	#Transform		#FactFri	

To pay or not to pay, that is the question

Facebook allows you to do campaigns where you purchase time to be in front of your potential client. I generally do not pay for Facebook marketing unless I am trying to get massive attention to an event I am hosting or to offer a coupon to clients to drum up business. Most people will find me through shares from my realtors and clients, and that is free marketing to their network.

Overall, Facebook marketing is very affordable. I've been able to get in front of 10,000 people locally, which 19 of them "Claimed my offer" where I was offering $100 off our 550 E-decorating service. This only cost me $130.00, which is an average $7.00 per claimed coupon. Of those 19 claimed coupons, 2 of them redeemed them which means I clearly made a profit by running this Facebook ad.

Best Times to Post on Social Media By:

Source	M	Tu	W	Th	Fri	Sat	Su	Times
Facebook (% of higher engagement)				X 19%	X 19%	X 32%	X 32%	Most clicks: 3pm Most shares: 1pm
Twitter			X					Biz2biz is best during business hours. Biz2client performs 17% better on weekends. Best times: 1pm & 5-6pm.
Linked In		X	X	X				Best times: 7:30-8:30am & 5-6pm.
Pinterest						X	X	Top topics: Sat-Travel, Sun-Food. Best times: 8-11pm.
Instagram	X		X					Posting videos on Instagram gets 34% more interactions. Best times: 2-3pm & 8-9pm.

Google	X	90% of people on Google+ are lurkers & will not interact with your content. Best times: 9-11am.

BEST DAYS FOR SPECIFIC MEDIA
More Networks = More Engagements[6]

Sunday – Facebook
> Primarily used on mobile & desktop at work and home.

Tuesday – Linked In
> Used for professionals around work hours.

Wednesday – Google+
> Targets work professionals with interactions in early AM.

Thursday – Instagram
> User platform is mobile so it's used anytime all the time.

Saturday – Pinterest
> Users like surfing at night while watching TV.

All Days – Twitter
> Most read are during down times like commutes & breaks.

BONUS: 40 min Training Video
A course I taught live to 100 attendees on how I got to 40 staging jobs per month in my business using social media.
https://www.youtube.com/watch?v=TRnLM-0kKzI&feature=youtu.be

---

[6] http://coschedule.com/blog/best-times-to-post-on-social-media/

Leverage & Hiring Tips.

Not Enough Hours In A Day

Many of you will agree that there are not enough hours in a day. Twenty-four hours just doesn't seem sufficient anymore with work, growing a business, raising a family, seeing friends, hobbies, networking, social events, charities, parties, etc. How do the sharks from the show "Shark Tank" have the time to run multiple companies? How does Richard Branson have the time to run the entire Virgin Empire that keeps expanding? Better yet, how does measly little me accomplish everything I've listed out in this book PLUS run another company and have time to take vacations with my family? One word......LEVERAGE!

A business cannot be built with just one person cause that would be defined as a self-made job. Which is fine if that is your goal in your business. You don't have to try and create an "empire" or a massive company, you can happily run one all by yourself and make good money. However, when it comes to selling that, it's not very appealing to potential investors. People with money who want to purchase businesses want to purchase a business that a) has potential for quick ROI (return on investment) and b) is generally fully operational without them, meaning they like to acquire income producing assets that require little to no work on their end. Now, this is not saying your small single person business is not sellable, it is and someone will buy it (generally another stager wanting to get into the business), but it will not be evaluated and worth the same as a business where the owner has taken the time to set up all the systems and get the necessary people in place and operational.

This is why the franchise model is so successful, you do not purchase a RE/MAX balloon brand if you want to have a horse as your logo. Realtor offices also understand the power of leverage. This is why the broker will have multiple agents working in the office. If one agent works 40hrs a week, then 10 agents make 400 hours. While the broker doesn't pay out the hourly fees, he does collect a % off each home sold. This is how people get rich and have time freedom; having other people take on tasks that will allow them to eventually become free.

WARNING

Creating your own leverage system will result in a structure that looks much like a "pyramid", but don't worry you are safe, nothing about leverage or even a "pyramid" is illegal. If you want to know what is illegal, email me because I've done a ton of research when learning about what is and is not illegal while I was looking up the company I work with for my legal services.

Tips for leverage

- Hire help
    - From assistants to administration, determine needs first.
- Have a system in place
    - Once this book is finished, you'll have the majority of what you need to train staff in specific parts of the company.
- Don't micromanage
    - Use your systems to train the staff. Outline that the end result is key and how it is done, especially if it's more efficient, is open for discussion.
- Have the right people in the right place
    - When hiring for office duties, make sure that is where their strong skills lie. An admin who wants to be a stager and decorator will not stay in this position for a long period of time because it's not where their passion lies.

Hiring Staff

Hiring staff can be exciting, stressful and expensive! Initially in this book, I outlined some general principles of "independent stagers" VS "staff stagers". You'll want to start by identifying which model is legal in your market and suits your goals for your business.

Your First Hire

Who should you hire first in your business? When I was working all hours of the day, evenings and Saturdays, I made a decision that my first hire would be another stager that will perform all evening & weekend consultations. This meant I would have to use the Home Staging system I created on how to perform our written consultation to train this person on how I wanted Capital Home Staging & Design to be represented. But don't fret because we already did this in a previous chapter based on your training and what you want to do as far as the style of consultations that work best for you. For me, my basic overview of a consult system was:

    1) Establish rapport with the client immediately (compliment them).
    2) Sit down to discuss selling goals & marketing plans.
    3) 10 min tour of the home with owners.
    4) 45 min tour of home writing down suggestions in our book.
    5) 20 min review and Q&A with the owners.
    6) 15 min email to realtors advising appointment is done and how it was received by the owners (happy, mad, annoyed,…).

This is all written out in a document that I review with my candidate and then I allow them to shadow me on a few appointments. I shadow them until we are both comfortable with their skills and they can go out on their own. Yes, you'll technically be paying double for the appointment because you'll want to be paid and the staff will want to be paid, but when you have a good hire, it's worth every penny to invest in time for the training process.

When I hire an evenings & weekends stager, I advise them that I do not ever guarantee hours, as it is dependent on the number of requests coming in each month. This sets the precedence that it's not within our control and they are guaranteed nothing but work when it comes in. So when it's slow and they complain that they want more hours, then you can remind them that you never guaranteed any type of work.

Once you have an established assistant, an evenings & weekends help, you'll be able to focus on daytime appointments and the necessary office work that all business owners have to work on.

Generally, the next hire is an office assistant and they are usually part time. Based on your needs, you can hire them for 2 full days a week if you really need help, e.g. every Monday & Thursday, or you can do Monday through Friday from 9am-12:00pm. It is harder to find staff for such short and frequent hours, unless you are hiring a stay-at-home mom or retiree who has a flexible schedule. Office assistants are designed to take tasks off of your plate so you can focus on what you do best. From answering phones, responding to emails, booking appointments, obtaining necessary paperwork per job before it reaches the stager for importation and so much more. This is why it is important to start writing slowly each office task you do and HOW you do it, because eventually when you are ready to have an administrator, you'll be able to train them only once by showing them and then telling them about the protocol in your "SOP binder" where they can look up the "how-to" of each task they are now managing.

How to Hire / Where to Look

This is the hardest part. WHERE oh WHERE do you find good employees that won't come and train with you and use your time just to up and leave in a year to give it a go on their own? Well you won't know, there is no guarantee, but there are general types of people that are less likely to do this to you:

- People who've had their own business in the past, but couldn't get it off the ground. They are generally talented stagers, but can't run a business properly.
- Retired men and women. Generally they feel they are too old to try and start off new in building and growing their own brand. This is not a true guarantee as I've met many retirees that chose to be independent, however they are mature enough to tell you that that is their plans.
- People who are well off financially. Normally, they are doing this with you as a hobby to them, but it helps your business. They don't do it for the money, they do it for the love of the creativity. This is a big asset since our industry is so unpredictable in jobs and you can't guarantee income.

When I am hiring, I post a position title and job duties on my webpage. I never post my pay range because I don't want unqualified people to apply just to make the income that's typically much higher than minimum wage. I also have tried posting on Kijiji and job forum sites, but end up only receiving bulk applications from desperate people looking for any job, which typically results in higher turnover as they will leave you when a better opportunity comes along. Stick to asking your network of realtors, design stores, college design students who are interested in the task at hand.

The biggest thing I learned when hiring for administrative help is to NEVER hire anyone for the position that is interested in being one of your future stagers. Some people will have different views on this than me, however in my experience, you just trained them on the administration followed by the staging side, so they see how your entire business works AND you'll also have to hire a new admin person when they do the transfer. Where if you find, hire and train a specific admin person who is only interested in that job, you'll just have to focus on hiring and training new staging staff while the designated administrator takes care of running the office for you.

Family, Friends & Strangers

How do you feel about working with your spouse? Parents? Brother or sister? Day in and day out? Some of you have amazing communication skills and can accomplish anything together, but for the bulk of us in the world, it's a set-up for pure disaster. I learned this from experience again, unfortunately.

When I needed administration, office and warehouse help, I hired many people part time and they all left because they wanted guaranteed full time hours at a salary of 40K and up, which is a lot of dough to a home staging company. So finally, my dad came up with the idea that I should hire my mom to do the administrative work because when they had a business (20+ years ago), she was very good on the phone and was able to get people sold and registered for their work. Therefore, I sat down with my mom and did an interview about her skills, asking her if she was able to multitask (she said yes because she was planning many events where she currently worked). I think that is awesome because in our industry, we need to multitask very well. We discussed phones, emails, document creating and many more.

After a contract and payment terms outlined, my mom quit her 40K job that provided her with benefits and a retirement plan to come work for me where I had no benefits or retirement plan in place. A CLEAR gamble on both of our parts to see how this would work out.

Flash forward 1 year into having her as part of my team, she wasn't accomplishing nearly as many tasks as I thought she would have because I was doing them, her mindset was very linear, and she couldn't truly multitask on FAST projects. Long term projects sure, she was a champ! It was the daily answering of phones and emails, booking appointments, getting paperwork and files in order, jumping from one client to another in a matter of minutes, which were clearly way too fast for her to manage without issues. This was a strong lesson to both of us on how to establish a clear communication for what I FEEL is multitasking and what the prospect FEELS as multitasking. When this is discussed in detail at the beginning, it avoids issues later.

So now I am in a pickle, a big fat messy pickle! I hired my mom, who QUIT her job that she enjoyed, to work for me at a salary I could barely afford; I figured with her FAST MULTITASKING ways (that I expected were to be like mine), I would be able to get more jobs and be able to afford her increased expense. Well that didn't happen, I still had to take on many office duties to ensure things were getting done while she managed what she could when she was working in the office. So what do I do????

We decided that it was best my mom be laid off so she could find employment elsewhere. Thank God my mother was understanding and knew that what I needed was best provided by someone else, and she didn't freak out on me or blame me or anything. This was a clear indicator for me on how interviews should be VERY specific about the skills you want paired with the skills the prospect has. You'll want to outline what you really require from someone on a specific task.

Some good questions for efficiency / productivity;
* Can you manage multiple files from multiple clients in a manner that they are completed fully and organized without mixing them up?
* Describe to me a time where you successfully managed multiple tasks in a short period of time. What were the results?
* How fast can you type? Are you good at spelling & grammar?
* Do you know how to operate xxxxxxx (list)?
* Have you ever had a situation where files were mixed up and the wrong service or product was delivered to a client? If so, how was it resolved?

Interview Process.

Most of you will have your own ways of hiring, but the key is to keep it consistent for each candidate so no one can claim an unfair advantage. This is my interview process:

1. **Review Resumes** – Anything that stands out as unique I will "Approve" for the next level, all others I will recycle or delete.
2. **Phone Interview** – I do this to reduce the amount of DUD meetings. I generally use it to get a scope on how the person communicates through a phone and how he / she responds general questions about the job. This will make or break a candidate based on her answers.
   a. Are you afraid of animals, reptiles or arachnids?
   b. Are you ok to work alone in other people's homes?
   c. Do you have reliable transportation?
   d. Can you lift 25-50 lbs with ease?
   e. Are you considered physically fit by a doctor?
   f. Do you have a required income goal you need to achieve?
   g. How do you like working alone? How do you like working with a team?

3. **In-person Interview** – After I've established the candidate meets the majority of the job's needs, I will meet them for an in-person interview to see how they dress and carry themselves professionally, if their nails are manicured, did they come prepared, and most importantly, WHY do they want to work for us and WHO are we? I want my prospects to Google and learn about us before they say they want to be hired by us. I also provide a TEST for all prospects I meet with. Essentially, I bring a BEFORE photo of an empty room and draw out the room's walls, doors, windows, and tell them what the price point of the home is and who the targeted buyer is. Then I ask them to draw out how they would furnish the space and tell me what it looks like as far as colour schemes, atmosphere, etc. This is a great technique to see someone's instincts. I can tell you, very rarely are people 100%

right without seeing the space in person, so don't be too hard on them, but you will know if they clearly have no idea what they are talking about.

4. **Shadowing Appointment** – Here, I get potential prospects to shadow me on one of my jobs, and as I'm working, I ask for their gut instincts on how they would prepare the room. This allows me to see more of their skill sets and how they are able to communicate their thoughts to me in a constructive way that makes sense.

5. **Decision & Job Offer with Probation** – Finally, after all the candidates have been interviewed, I review all the information, select one of them and provide them with a job offer letter and a contract (written by an employment lawyer), outlining that probation is 6 months or 300 hours of work, whichever comes first. After that period, we will sit down for a review and either extend the contract to permanent part time work or terminate the relationship at this point. All of our trainings during the probationary period is PAID training, but I only pay them minimum wage at this point.

Notes for Staff Growth

Paying Staff / Structure

A pay structure will vary based on the area you live in as well as if your business can afford to pay in these brackets. Meaning, if your 2hr consultation is only $100 and you have to pay a minimum of 3hrs for any staff member, or if they hit 10+ years of employment in your company and you pay your staff $120, but only made $100, you would be running a negative deficit business. It will not survive! Here's an example of our pay structure based on longevity:

Employed For	Hourly Wage
0-6 months (probation)	Minimum Wage
6 months-1 year	$15/hour
1-5 years	$16-25/hr (based on skills)
5-9 years	$26-35/hr (based on skills)
10 yrs +	$40/hr

Another factor you need to consider when paying teammates is mileage fees. It is MUCH cheaper to purchase a company car for them to use than pay out insane mileage fees for each job. Staff rarely go the most direct route and tend to stop for personal tasks. It's impossible to track properly as well. With my team, since they are at each consult for 2hrs and I pay them for 3hrs, the last hour we feel is value enough for their travel time to and from each job. Even if the next appointment is next door, they are paid for 3 hours. In the long run, it generally comes out in the wash that the 3rd hour essentially compensates for the drive time to each job.

I know some stagers in North America who did the mileage payment method and it nearly destroyed their business. Many staff do not understand that companies which pay mileage do so because they CAN afford to, they may also have government assistance as some business qualify for those benefits. Just because one company pays out mileage DOES NOT mean your company should too if you cannot afford to do so.

Our Overall Pay Structure For Staff

Consultations	3hrs per consult (no more / no less)
Vacant Small Job	hourly with a cap at 10 hours
Vacant Large Job	hourly with a cap at 24 hours

For all jobs I quote, I invoice clients for the maximum projected hours to complete the job. If staff finish quickly, I can give them a bonus or if I spend a lot on inventory, it can go to paying off that initial investment.

Congratulations On Completing Your Core Business Systems!

Kristy Morrison

Resources

Select PDF Documents Outlined In This Book:
http://www.kristymorrison.com/#!book-resources/cpm1y
Log In Password: StagingSystems

Agendas:
I love paper agendas, it really helps with time blocking.

I prefer the use of the **passionplanner.com**
Referral Code: **kristy@chsd.ca**

Appliance & Home Systems Protection Plans:
Canada Appliance & Home Systems Protection Plan.
Benefits: Peace of mind and security of home systems.
Eric Bowen: 613-897-7467 | **EricB@restorahome.ca**
www.RestoraHome.ca

Catherine Lewis Brown:
Why work with me? Because I love to see stagers succeed! And because I've been in stager's shoes. I'm a staging business owner, but I'm also an International Master Stager, past CSP staging trainer and now creater of my own training programs.

After three years training and mentoring stagers, and learning where they stumble, I decided I wanted to created online programs, tools & resources especially that would inspire, motivate & empower stagers to achieve the greatness they deserve. No more stumbling!!

I am so passionate about seeing stagers succeed that my first online program does just that! Check out **'8-Weeks To A Successful Staging Biz!,'** plus these six (and more to come) stand alone **Stager MasterClasses**. Each program builds on existing skill sets, introduces best practices and creates an environment that nurtures stager's mindset!

- o Nail the Consultation!

- o The Decorating Fundamentals of Staging
- o Be the Vacant Staging Expert
- o Demystifying Pricing, Quotes and Contracts
- o Adding Staging to Your Business
- o How To Find The Ideal Client

For more information, please email me at Catherine@catherinelewisbrown.com or text or call 289-356-2642. You can check out all our programs at www.catherinelewisbrown.com.

Like my Facebook page https://www.facebook.com/catherinelewisbrowntraining/

And don't forget to sign-up for my free e-tools!

Dropbox:
https://db.tt/OhoC371
Earn up to 16GB of FREE STORAGE!

FinanceScapes:
Receive 25% off your order to assist with your cash flow evaluator.

James Fellows: help@finanscapes.com
www.finanscapes.com Coupon Code: StagingSystems

Fiverr:
Resource where you can literally get anything designed for about $5.00. One of the designers created my first book cover so you can see they are very professional in what they do.

FREE Evaluation of Business Systems:
Wholesale pricing for home & business owners.
Phones, Internet, Cell Phones, Gas, Electricity, Solar, Merchant Processing, Security Systems/Automation, Hot Water Tanks, TV & More. **KeTeam.Services4u.com**
What do you have to lose with a free evaluation?

Home Staging Training:
APSD – Association of Property Scene Designers (online)
http://apsdmembers.com/homestagingtraining/
kristymorrison/

Legal Set-Up Plan:
Eric Delorme: 613-868-9976 (cell) | edelorme@rogers.com

Merchant Processing:
Anovia Credit Card Processing: Free quotes.
KeTeam.Services4u.com

MyDarby Inventory Programs:
www.mydarby.com Referral Code: CHSD

Newsletters Tool:
mailchimp.com is a tool I've used where I can send 2000 emails in 1 month for free.
wix.com has this tool as well.

Social Media Automation: www.Hootsuite.com

Social Media Posts:
www.Canva.com (Free account) some bonus layouts and photos are available for purchase.

Stager Association:
RESA: www.RealEstateStagingAssociation.com

Webpage Creation:
wix.com is one of the EASIEST platforms I've ever used. I recently transferred all of my webpages from Word Press over to Wix because of how easy it is to edit and navigate. They offer thousands and thousands of templates to customize.
Examples: KristyMorrison.com &
CapitalHomeStagingAndDesign.ca

Work With Kristy

Kristy is working on a very unique and out-of-the-box project alongside her staging business with great success. She is looking for open-minded and passionate people who want to work together.

This project may be for you if…

- You are interested in streamlining your staging **income** to offset the slow season without increasing your expenses.
- You'd like to become **cutting edge** in your local market.
- You want a unique way to **book meetings** with more realtors & office presentations.
- You want to obtain **more free time** in your life for the things you love like family and friends.
- You like meeting like-minded, goal-orientated professionals that empower and help each other.
- You are interested in working **side by side with Kristy** on an exciting project that is helping thousands of people across North America in a way that doesn't take time away from our business.

If you answered YES to any of the above statements, then you are like Kristy in her thought process and she would love to chat with you to see if your goals and her goals line up. If they do, Kristy will send you a link to a private page with an access code where you'll watch a 35 min project overview video. You'll have the entire project laid out for a thorough evaluation.

Together we can accomplish so much.

To schedule a call,
KristyMorrison0@gmail.com
SUBJECT: Let's work together.

My Social Media

Facebook
/BusinessSystemsForStagers
(this book)

/CapitalHomeStagingAndDesign
(staging business)

/Kristy.MorrisonBowen
(personal page)

/KristyMorrison.CHSD
(new business building page)

Twitter
@CapitalHStaging
@OttawaStager

Instagram
LadyBossOttawa

Linked In
Kristy Morrison

Other Publications

Author: Kristy Morrison

Competitive Edge: Transforming Your Home And Maximizing Profits Through Real World Home Staging Cases.

Competitive Edge is an extremely comprehensive book, covering all of the important aspects of home staging. It is a must-read, particularly for anyone looking to gain their "competitive edge" when selling their greatest asset. Kristy does a wonderful job of making this an easy read by offering fun, real world examples, step by step tips, and case studies that help to clear up any misconceptions you may have about staging. This book educates you on the various options available to home sellers, and offers great advice on selling and marketing in a variety of real estate markets. Selling real estate has become fast-paced with ever changing strategies required to ensure top dollar; this book provides that valuable insight into the thought process of the almighty buyer. This is a well-written book by an internationally recognized home staging professional simply looking to give you the upper hand when selling what could be your most valuable asset.

For sale on amazon.ca & amazon.com under the book title. Autographed copies available through KristyMorrison.com

1 of 2 people found the following review helpful

⭐⭐⭐⭐⭐ **Awesome book for Home Owners, Realtors, and Home Stagers!** May 27 2014

By **Sherri** - Published on Amazon.com

Format: Paperback   **Verified Purchase**

This book is designed to help home owners prepare their homes to sell fast and for the most amount of money, BUT it is a great resource for Home Stagers too! Kristy does a great job explaining what needs to be done in each room of a home to give it that "Competitive Edge" which can be seen in the photos PLUS the website she provides with color photos. Love it! Realtors can read this book for help talk to home owners that have "objections" to paying for a home stager. Home Stagers....use it for great verbiage when speaking to your potential clients to get more business. Home Sellers...listen closely to what Kristy is telling you if you want to sell your home QUICKLY and if you want to keep YOUR profit from your biggest investment. Buy the book now, I'm glad I did! Thanks Kristy!

Education & Awards

Algonquin College
Veterinary Technician
(I personally use this skill to connect
with home owners -pet tips)

QC Design School
International Staging & Redesign Professional
Professional Organizer
Interior Decorating

APSD Training
Home Stager
Stager Pro
Master Trainer -APSD Canada

School of Trial & Error
Nothing will prepare you for the business world
most of your success will be a result of
trial and error.

RESA Member Since 2008

Awards / Accomplishments
2016 -RESA Convention Speaker
2015 -Top 10 Home Staging Team RESA
2014 -Top 10 Professional Stager Canada -RESA
2014 -RESA Convention Speaker
2013 -Top 10 Professional Stager -RESA
2012 -2nd place Company of the Year Canada -RESA
2010-Rookie Stager of the Year Finalist -RESA
2009- BBB TorchAward Winner
2009 -Staged For Suzanne Somers

About The Author

Kristy Morrison, founder of Capital Home Staging & Design – Ottawa's first award-winning home staging company, wrote her first book *Competitive Edge* in 2014 for realtors and homeowners to learn about the importance of preparing their property prior to selling, always with the view of getting a quick and profitable sale.

Too many see the value, but do not utilize it in their marketing plan, which is what Kristy wants to directly change. Faced with a difficult time selling one of her own properties, she vowed to take what she had learned and use it to help other home owners avoid losing thousands of dollars from their greatest asset, their home.

Her next book, **Creating Successful Business Systems: A Home Staging & Decorators Guide,** was a labor of love after #RESACon2016 where Kristy was a featured speaker on setting up your business for success with systems. She had a packed room with stagers from all over the world, which resulted in a massive outcry for more help with getting their systems up and running. With a great suggestion from a local stager to write a book, she took it upon herself to deliver.

Kristy loves to continually learn about changing aspects in the staging industry. Graduating from a local college with four different diplomas, she has established a focus on where she wanted to be in business. In 2010, Kristy attended an APSD Home Staging Conference in Denver, Colorado and was blown away. Subsequently, Kristy expanded her training and worked her way up to becoming an APSD Certified Master Trainer. This certification allows her to teach the cutting edge home staging techniques to stagers across Canada.

Since opening up Capital Home Staging & Design and becoming number one in the local market, Kristy has been featured in a published staging book called *"Unforgettable Spaces, I discover home staging"* by Stephanie Lyca, as well as numerous publications such as: The Ottawa Citizen's Real Deal section, various real estate websites, Marketwire online publication, London Free Press and much more. Kristy has also been featured on the cover of the Ottawa Carleton District School Board's magazine, for her course offering in adult education. Furthermore, she has been a monthly guest speaker on Rogers TV talking about various elements in the staging industry and an annual guest speaker at Home Staging Conferences nationally, speaking about the home staging business and the potential for others to grow their own business just as she has.

Kristy currently lives in Ottawa, Ontario with her husband and fur babies Marley, Buster, Boscoe & Smokey. As an entrepreneur that loves a challenge, she runs many companies that are outlined on her webpage. When she is not working, you can find her reading a business book at the cottage or renovating and changing decor frequently in her home (much to her husband's annoyance!).

www.KristyMorrison.com

 Goodreads Author